Being on Fire

Being on Fire

THE TOP TEN ESSENTIALS OF CATHOLIC FAITH

by

Richard G. Malloy, S.J.

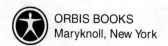
ORBIS BOOKS
Maryknoll, New York

ORBIS BOOKS
Maryknoll, New York 10545

Fathers and Brothers
MARYKNOLL™

Founded in 1970, Orbis Books endeavors to publish works that enlighten the mind, nourish the spirit, and challenge the conscience. The publishing arm of the Maryknoll Fathers and Brothers, Orbis seeks to explore the global dimensions of the Christian faith and mission, to invite dialogue with diverse cultures and religious traditions, and to serve the cause of reconciliation and peace. The books published reflect the views of their authors and do not represent the official position of the Maryknoll Society. To learn more about Maryknoll and Orbis Books, please visit our website at www.maryknollsociety.org.

Manufactured in the United States of America.

Library of Congress Cataloging-in-Publication Data

Malloy, Richard G.
Being on fire : the top ten essentials of Catholic faith / Richard G. Malloy.
     pages   cm
     Includes bibliographical references.
     ISBN 978-1-62698-070-9 (pbk.)
     1. Catholic Church—Doctrines. 2. Theology, Doctrinal—Popular works. I. Title.
BX1754.M2685   2014
230'.2—dc23

                                        2013037516

To Fr. Henry B. Haske, S.J. (1927-2012), Loyola High School football star, missionary, Jesuit leader, mentor, and spiritual director extraordinaire, my deepest gratitude for all you gave and taught us. And to all those of the long, black line of the Society of Jesus, who, like Henry, have given all of their talents, treasure, and time to the work of the church and the kingdom of God. And to Leo E. Ryan, Jr. (1933-2010), husband of Katie and father of eight, a man who enjoyed life and loved God, his family, and his friends. Both Leo and Henry were true fathers to me and to so many.

Deo Gratias

Be who God meant you to be and you will set the world on fire
—Catherine of Siena

Contents

You touched me, and I am set on fire to attain the peace which is yours.

—St. Augustine, *Confessions*

Words of wisdom from Charles Schulz's Peanuts: Snoopy is sitting on his doghouse, typing on his typewriter. Charlie Brown says, "I hear you're writing a book on Theology. I hope you have a good title." Snoopy thinks, "I have the perfect title . . . 'Has It Ever Occurred to You That You Might Be Wrong?'"

Preface

Some nights I stay up cashing in my bad luck
Some nights I call it a draw
Some nights I wish that my lips could build a castle
Some nights I wish they'd just fall off

But I still wake up, I still see your ghost
Oh, Lord, I'm still not sure what I stand for, oh,
What do I stand for? What do I stand for?
Most nights I don't know anymore . . .
                                         —Indie Rock Group FUN

Call her Mia. She just graduated from the University of Scranton where she immersed herself in academic pursuits, majoring in sociology and theology. She played volleyball and worked on several local community service projects. She spent a semester at the Casa de Solidaridad in El Salvador, mastering Spanish and expanding her horizons in multiple directions and depths. She is doing a post-graduation year as a Jesuit Volunteer working with homeless women and children in Houston. Mia knows where she stands and for what she stands.

Call him Mike. He comes into my office. He's down and distressed. College in many ways is wonderful for him. His grades are good and he has many friends. But he's still not happy. "Fr. Rick, I just don't know what I believe. I wish I could go to Mass more and get on another retreat, but I just end up partying and messing up. I don't know what's wrong with me. I just don't know anymore." Mike doesn't know where he stands or for what he stands.

This book is for those who know where they stand and also for those who "don't know anymore." They may have heard the gospel, but they don't know what they stand for. They find themselves in the darkness of night, and they deeply desire to wake up and walk in the light of day. They just don't know how. God wants to show us the way. God wants to give us the gifts of faith and hope and love. God wants us to receive the power to be courageous persons, prudent persons, temperate persons, men and women who do justice. God's spirit can make us wise, understanding, and reverent, filled with knowledge and fortitude, men and women who are in awe of the wonder and love of God. Mia is further along in that process than Mike.

In 1978, Scott Peck's best seller *The Road Less Traveled* appeared and spent several years on the New York Times best-seller list. It begins with the words "Life is difficult." Our culture needed to hear those words, because too many think that life's inevitable tragedy means God is absent or uncaring. Although there are inevitable trials and tribulations in everyone's life, our faith tells us life is wonderful and wacky, promising and powerful. Life is to be lived lovingly and to the fullest. Jesus came that we might "have life and have it abundantly" (John 10:10). Yet too many are missing the memo. Life, if not "nasty, brutish, and short," is stressful, painful, and meaningless for many of our brothers and sisters. In a world that many would consider paradise (we eat; we are clothed; we have hot showers and flush toilets—all the stuff of dreams for most of human history and for billions on our planet in our times), many are soul sick, deeply depressed, distressed, and, in a word, lost. Too many of the young people I meet as a campus minister are unhappy and unfulfilled. I see too many Mikes and too few Mias. The Mikes are searching for something that can give their lives meaning and mission, peace and promise. Many of the cups they are offered are filled with anything but the nourishment they need. They are like the guy in this joke.

There's this guy at a bar, just looking at his drink. He stays like that for half of an hour. Then, this big trouble-making truck driver steps next to him, takes the drink from the guy, and just drinks it all down. The poor man starts crying. The truck driver says, "Come on man,

I was just joking. Here, I'll buy you another drink. I just can't stand to see a man cry." The guy replies, "No, it's not that. This day is the worst of my life. First, I fall asleep, and I get to work late. My boss, all ticked off, fires me. When I leave the building, I go to my car, and I find out it's been stolen. The police say that they can't do anything. I get a cab home, and as the cab drives away, I realize I left my wallet and credit cards in the back seat. When I get into the house, I find my wife in bed with the gardener. I left home and came to this bar. And just when I was thinking about putting an end to my life, you show up and drink my poison."

We don't have to drink the poisons of our age. Our God wants to give us grace, the power to do what we could not do before. God wants us to live happy and healthy and holy and free. We need to open our minds and hearts to God's power and presence. Doing so will set us quietly alight, on fire with the beauty, truth, wisdom, compassion and goodness of God. That's what we need and want. That's what our world wants and needs, people inspired and inspiring.

In this book, I describe Catholicism's Top Ten Essentials. So many reject the Catholic faith and the practices of Catholicism because they disagree with this or that teaching of the church. But those teachings make no sense if you don't know the basics. The practice of touching all the bases makes no sense until you understand what baseball is. Then a ball hit out of the park is cause for joy as the Phillies' Ryan Howard trots around the diamond and heads home. Understand Catholicism's "Top Ten" and a lot more about our faith will make sense. Catholicism is all about creating a world where we can enjoy life and live free, free from all that oppresses us, free for all that makes life wonderful, free "to love tenderly, do justice, and walk humbly with our God" (Micah 6:8).

True and transformative religion and sane spirituality make us free persons, not slaves. "For freedom Christ has set us free" (Gal 5:1). Richard Rohr teaches that true freedom is not the license to do whatever you want. Real freedom is wanting to do what you need and ought to do (Rohr 2003, 108). Real religion isn't a brake on our emotional or intellectual development. In fact, religion, when practiced sanely and well, is actually a catalyst for transformation into the fullness of human living and being.

Multitudes of young adults religiously reject faith, as if it were their job. They think religion imposes rules and regulations on them, won't allow them to think freely, and, frankly, just wants to get their money. Recent research finds the opposite. Religion is actually "good for you." T. M. Luhrmann has found that church

> boosts the immune system and decreases blood pressure. It may add as much as two to three years to your life. . . . Social support is no doubt part of the story. At the evangelical churches I've studied as an anthropologist, people really did seem to look out for one another. They showed up with dinner when friends were sick and sat to talk with them when they were unhappy. The help was sometimes surprisingly concrete. . . . Healthy behavior is no doubt another part. Certainly many churchgoers struggle with behaviors they would like to change, but on average, regular church attendees drink less, smoke less, use fewer recreational drugs and are less sexually promiscuous than others. That tallies with my own observations. (Lurhmann 2013)

Luhrmann chronicles how churches help people really change destructive dynamics in their lives. Many she interviewed related how they found God and got off drugs like methamphetamine. "One woman told me that while cooking her dose, she set off an explosion in her father's apartment and blew out his sliding glass doors. She said to me, 'I knew that God was trying to tell me I was going the wrong way' " (Lurhmann 2013). She also found some humor in churches. "In my next church, I remember sitting in a house group listening to a woman talk about an addiction she could not break. I assumed that she was talking about her own struggle with methamphetamine. It turned out that she thought she read too many novels" (Lurhmann 2013). Luhrmann goes on to note the pain of those who want to be close to God but cannot find ways to establish or maintain the relationship. She notes the tragic case of famous mega-church pastor Rick Warren's son, who committed suicide. Church isn't magic. We Christians tell a true story of a crucified God, a God who is with us in our sufferings and in our joys.

We are the stories we tell, and without good stories, our lives cannot be fulfilled or give us a sense of transcendence, the felt experience of living within and for something greater than ourselves. Without stories that help us name and claim our destiny and meaning, we find it hard to simply live, let alone live happy and healthy and holy and free. Our demythologized world has left us without stories to orient and guide us. How did we go from *It's a Wonderful Life* in 1946 to *American Beauty* in 1999? Lester Burnham, with his sad and sorrowful midlife crisis, is a paltry substitute for George Bailey's life of innate courage, self-sacrifice, and community centeredness. *The Big Bang Theory* and *Two and a Half Men* are not parables worth modeling our lives on. Bill Cosby's *The Huxtables* and the Camdens of *7th Heaven* are better role models for us and our children. *The West Wing* television series spoke of the honor, grace, and moral challenges of serving in government; Netflix's *House of Cards* has Congressman Frank Underwood (Kevin Spacey) manipulating people ruthlessly and without any concern for the well-being of others, let alone the common good. Politics, for Underwood, is just a game of power. Catholicism, at best, is a series of stories that teach us how to live and serve and find meaning and purpose in our lives. The practices of our faith can set our hearts on fire with passion for prayer, serenity, for service, and love for life.

The deeper problem is the watered down sense of spirituality and religion, and thus the diminished sense of self and God experienced by so many in our age of "do it yourself religion" (see Taylor 2007). A God whom we tailor to our self-centered desires, a God who makes no demands, cannot promise transcendence or a life-sustaining sense of purpose and meaning. The only way to really have a deeply felt and thought-through sense of who God is, and who I and we are in relation to God, is to give and entrust oneself to a religious tradition over a lifetime. You can't be a Philadelphia Eagles fan for one or two seasons and really experience the joy and pandemonium that will erupt if "da Birds" ever win the Super Bowl. It's the same with God. You cannot have what religion and sane spirituality offer without long-term commitment. The phenomenon of frequent switching, which dominates our cultural mode of relating to God, weakens a felt sense of deep meaning in connection to our religious practices. One is born Catholic, drifts away from religion in one's late teens and early twenties, lives with someone, may marry, finds a church with a likable, inoffensive pastor when kids come along, and dabbles in yoga or Eastern spiritualities from time to time, or returns to the faith traditions of one's youth, or just drifts through life on an amorphous sense of being "spiritual but not religious."

> Despite the frequent claim that we are living in a secular age defined by the death of God, many citizens in rich Western democracies have merely switched one notion of God for another—abandoning their singular, omnipotent (Christian or Judaic or whatever) deity reigning over all humankind and replacing it with a weak but all-pervasive idea of spirituality tied to a personal ethic of authenticity and a liturgy of inwardness. The latter does not make the exorbitant moral demands of traditional religions, which impose bad conscience, guilt, sin, sexual inhibition and the rest. (Critchley and Webster 2013)

The real problem is that weak religion and surface spirituality often fail to provide the sustenance needed to meet the demands of life and love. God who is love doesn't just ask us to love one another. God demands that we love one another. God made us dependent on one another. One Christmas Eve, the great pastor the Rev. Martin Luther King Jr. said, "We will all need to learn to love one another as brothers and sisters, or we will perish like fools" (King 1967). The truth is we are all interconnected. "It really boils down to this: that all life is interrelated. We are all caught in an inescapable network of mutuality, tied into a single garment of destiny. Whatever affects one directly, affects all indirectly. We are made to live together because of the interrelated structure of reality" (King 1967).

It really boils down to this: that all life is interrelated. We are all caught in an inescapable network of mutuality, tied into a single garment of destiny. Whatever affects one directly, affects all indirectly. We are made to live together because of the interrelated structure of reality.

Prescient Thomas Merton had his prayer-filled sense focused on these problems years ago. He writes:

The whole problem of our time is the problem of love: how are we going to recover the ability to love ourselves and to love one another? The reason why we hate one another and fear one another is that we secretly or openly hate and fear our own selves. And we hate ourselves because the depths of our being are a chaos of frustration and spiritual misery. Lonely and help-less, we cannot be at peace with others because we are not at peace with ourselves, and we cannot be at peace with ourselves because we are not at peace with God. (Merton 1956, xii)

The essentials of our faith are that God loves us and wants to give us the power to love ourselves and others. God wants to set us on fire with the transformative grace of the Holy Spirit and the radical and revolutionary example of Jesus. God wants to give us what Mia has found and rejoiced in; God wants to show Mike where we stand. God wants us to form a church community that will bring order to the chaos and frustration of our turbulent religious and cultural lives. God deeply desires that we live and love, and learn how to do both. God wants to grace/gift us with joy for the journey, courage for the choices, faith for the freeing, hope for the healing, and love for the lasting.

At World Youth Day in Brazil 2013, the Jesuit Superior General, Adolfo Nicolas, S.J., spoke to young people about a Cambodian bishop who took a giraffe as a symbol of his diocese because the giraffe has the largest heart of all in the animal kingdom. It needs a big heart to pump blood up to its brain. He noted that the giraffe also has a higher viewpoint and can see beyond divisions and difficul-ties so apparent to those seeing on a lower level. "Humanity is more than any one of us has experienced in our own countries," Nicolas told the young people. He said that meeting others "with a big heart and a broad view can change their lives." He also told the young pil-grims, "Some people want to hold on to ancient traditions which say nothing to you young people. And many young people don't come to church and the older people say, 'They have no faith.' But I say, 'Yes, they have faith. Look at their hearts. There you will find it. God says to us that there is nothing complicated about the faith, but you must listen to your heart'" (CNS 2013).

Let's listen in the prayerful silence of the presence of God and allow the Holy Spirit to set our hearts on fire. "When the day of Pentecost had come . . . tongues of fire appeared among them, and a tongue rested on each of them. And they were filled with the Holy Spirit and began to speak" (Acts 2:1). Let's set the world ablaze with the transformative love and selfless compassion of God.

Introduction

"Ite, inflammate omnia" (*Go forth and set the world on fire*).
—The words of St. Ignatius Loyola as he sent Jesuits
on mission, especially those like St. Francis Xavier,
who were sent to faraway lands

There is ancient story of the Desert Fathers from the third century. A younger monk came to the older monk and shared how he fasted, prayed, and strived to live a life of heroic asceticism. He then asked the elder, what more should I do? The elder stretched out his hand and his fingers turned into ten lit lamps. "Why not become fire?"

> *Jesus was not just concerned with souls. He wanted a changed society.*
>
> —Lohfink, *Jesus of Nazareth,* 52

Pentecost should be as big a day in our spiritual lives as Christmas and Easter. We are filled with the Holy Spirit of love and that is symbolized by fire. In the Jesuit headquarters in Rome, there is a statue of St. Ignatius urging all to go and set the world on fire (ironically, a fire extinguisher stands right behind the statue). Being on fire is the gift of the Holy Spirit we deeply desire, a relationship with God is that for which we are made. To live as Jesus did, on fire with the Spirit of God, will fill us with purpose and peace. Our hearts hunger to be on fire. We want perpetual Pentecost. Being on fire will attract others to the living of our faith.

In *The Hunger Games*, Katniss captivates the capitol by appearing as the Girl on Fire. Our practice of Catholicism can fill us with the power of the Holy Spirit and should make us glow in ways that let all our brothers and sisters in the world know that God loves us and that the universe is user-friendly. As Catholics we are baptized to be like Jesus, open, inclusive, challenging, and willing and able to live out our lives as he did, always patterning ourselves after his life and ministry of self-sacrificing, transformative love.

Despite all the negative news of the past decades about priest pedophiles and incompetent to criminal bishops, the church continues to be a servant community. If you had told me in the year 2000 the revelations that were going to hit the headlines in the next ten years, I would have figured it was time to go get my truck driver's license and look for new work. Given the accounts of victims' pain and suffering, the inability of church authorities to defend the children, and the billions paid for therapy, reparations, and lawyers, it is amazing to me that the church is doing as well as we are. Personally, I am grateful for the ways people treat me knowing I am a priest. The vast majority realize it was 4 percent of priests involved in the scandals (USSCB 2011). Many people are still willing to listen to priests preach and to allow us to preside at baptisms and weddings and to be with them when loved ones enter eternal life. I live in a college dorm filled with first-year students, and parents and students are happy I am there, present as a resource for those adjusting to college and young adult life.

Despite all the trials and turbulence of the past few decades, the sixty-five or so million Catholics in this country make up a church that is still the largest private provider of social services in the nation. Public institutions tremble at the thought of the Catholic Church going out of business. Our Catholic communities' network of schools, hospitals, soup kitchens, family centers, and a myriad of other ministries endures despite all the evidence of sin and insanity in our midst. There are millions of Catholics in the United States muddling through every day, living out their baptismal vows in forms of prayer and service. From the "Eucharistic Adoration Catholics" to the "Mom and Pop and Three Kids Catholics," to the "Faith and Social Justice Catholics" to the "Christers" (seen only at Christmas and Easter), to the amazing influx of enthusiasm and energy provided by the growing Latinos among us (50 percent of Catholics under the age of twenty-five are Latinos), the church is, in ways mysterious and meaningful, a font of grace and a source of service for millions. The "Nuns on the Bus" charm some politicians and the media as they exemplify the best the Catholic Church has to offer. Little kids continue to tremble with excitement on the day of their First Communion, and may God help us do whatever is necessary to see that they are never again violated by pedophiles among us.

Yale professor Paul Kennedy, one of the few faculty members known to be a practicing Catholic at that prestigious institution, argues that, despite all the negative news, the church is alive and vibrant. He describes the Yale Catholic community's work with the poor and marginalized.

> The helpers at the soup kitchen are all volunteers; they would never expect to be remunerated. Not everyone is Catholic, but most are. They are the parishioners who live around Yale and come in for Sunday Mass and collegiality. They are the Yale students who also work in the downtown evening soup kitchen, or

in the men's overflow night shelter. A number of them are going off to Guatemala in mid-March to help rebuild a village still hurting from the civil wars. They welcome guest speakers and participate in theological discussion groups. This is not a dead or decaying church. It is vibrant and pulsing, rejoicing also in the beauty of the services (especially the sung Masses) and the sheer intellectualism of the homilies. It is *our* Catholic Church. Nobody is leaving it. (Kennedy 2013)

As Fr. Andrew Greeley once said, the clergy has done so much to try to make the laity leave, but they haven't succeeded. People keep coming back. And the church is flourishing in other parts of the world.

There are 1.2 billion people on our planet who call themselves Roman Catholic. That's 17.5 percent of the 7 billion plus people who populate earth. The number of priests worldwide has increased since 2000, and for fifteen years the numbers of seminarians has also risen. The church grew by 29 percent from 1990 to 2010. The church grew by 109 percent in Africa and in Asia by 50 percent (Wooden 2013). A recent PBS special reports that there are over 300 million Christians in China. The Fr. Zhangs of the twentieth-century persecutions are gazing upon us from heaven, seeing the flame of faith fanned from the embers they kept burning during their sufferings (see Wu 2004).

Demographic trends (see Saenz 2005) show that the church is far from dying. Projections for 2025 and 2050 indicate that we have many reasons to hope for a vibrant church in years to come.

Still, despite this growth, there are puzzling permutations. The Catholic population has grown tremendously, but vocations to the priesthood and religious life have not kept pace. In 1970 there were 419,728 priests and 1,004,304 religious sisters worldwide. In 2012 there were 412,236 priests and 721,935 sisters. In 1965 in the United States there were 58,632 priests and 179,954 sisters; in 2012, there were 38,964 priests and 54,018 sisters (CARA 2013). While baptisms across the world are numerous, there is often a lack of corresponding First Communions and Confirmations in later years. One in three raised Catholic in the United States is no longer Catholic,

	Number of Catholics	
	2025	*2050*
Latin America & Caribbean	568 Million	646 Million
Europe	272 Million	256 Million
Africa	219 Million	342 Million
Asia	172 Million	207 Million
North America	97 Million	113 Million
Oceania	11 Million	13 Million
World Wide	1.34 Billion	1.57 Billion

Saenz 2005

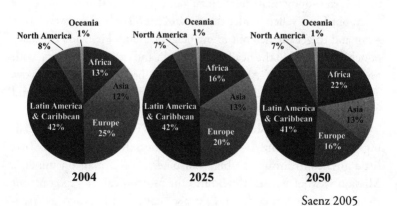

Saenz 2005

making former Catholics the second largest "religious" grouping in the United States. Lay leadership in the church will certainly have to increase in coming years, and those leaders will have to be on fire with the desire to sustain and build up the church. We need people to carry on the mission of Jesus Christ.

There is a story about a little guy who dies and arrives at the Pearly Gates. St. Peter looks in his book and says, "Dude, you really didn't do anything all that bad, but I really don't see anything good here that you did. Can you tell me some good deed you did in your lifetime?" The guy goes, "Sure. Once I was fishing in this park and I saw these two young people sitting on a bench holding hands, gazing at the sunset. All of a sudden, a gang of bikers, about a dozen of them, pull in behind the bench, and jump off their motorcycles. They begin beating the hell out of the guy and it looked like they were going to take advantage of the girl. To stop her being raped, and him being beaten to death, I ran to the back of my car, grabbed a lug wrench, and ran over to the crowd. I sized up the leader, a big monster biker, 6'5", 280 lbs., his neck all covered in tattoos and wearing a black leather jacket with silver studs, black jeans, and black motorcycle boots. I walked over to him and yelled at him to leave the young man and woman alone. He looked at me like I was crazy, but I just yelled louder that he and his biker buddies were pond scum and to get the hell out of my neighborhood. He made a fist and punched me hard in the head. I went down and came up swinging with my lug wrench. He . . ." At this point St. Peter breaks in and says, "Wow. That really took a great deal of courage to confront that gang. When did all this happen?" The guy replies, "Oh, about ten minutes ago."

The little guy probably should have yelled to the bikers he was calling 911, but sometimes we have to put ourselves on the line. That little guy, confronting the big, bad bikers, was a man on mission. Mission is what we are all about. Our mission calls us to confront the bad guys, as Moses did in Egypt so many centuries ago, as Archbishop Óscar Romero did in our times. Our mission calls us to celebrate life and make life possible for the poor. Our mission calls us to confront oppressors and other immoral powers. Think of the twenty-seven million mostly women enslaved in the sex industry today (see

Kristof and WuDunn 2009, 9) and of the millions of children forced to labor long hours for miniscule pay. The great liberation theologian Jon Sobrino, S.J., notes that the question isn't, "Does the church have a mission?" The question is, "Does the mission have a church?"

The mission of the church is clear: that the kingdom come. The will of God is clear: that the kingdom come. The purpose and meaning of the practice of the Catholic faith and the living of Catholic spirituality are clear: that the kingdom come. The reign of God is what Jesus preached, who Jesus was and is, and what we strive to be as the Body of Christ, the pilgrim people on the way to transformation in Christ. The reign of God leads to transformation of both our personal and social worlds.

> The obligation to commit oneself to the development of peoples is not just an individual duty, and still less an individualistic one, as if it were possible to achieve this development through the isolated efforts of each individual. It is an imperative which obliges each and every man and woman, as well as societies and nations. In particular, it obliges the Catholic Church and the other Churches and Ecclesial Communities, with which we are completely willing to collaborate in this field. (John Paul II, *On Social Concerns* §32)

Some called on mission give their lives for the cause of the reign of God. Since 1975, when the Society of Jesus articulated our mission as "the service of faith of which the promotion of justice is an absolute requirement" (General Congregation 32, §48), fifty-two Jesuits have been martyred. The best known are the six Jesuits and their cook and her daughter, November 16, 1989, in El Salvador. There are countless other Christians, and men and women of other faith traditions, who have given their lives in struggles for truth and justice. Their witness bolsters and challenges our faith. Our Catholic way of life calls us not only to confront evil, but to pray and strive in ways that carry us through evil to the glory of transformation and resurrection. Right after stating the Jesuit mission as the promotion of justice, the Society went on to say, "For reconciliation with God demands the reconciliation of people with one another" (General Congregation 32, §48).

Reconciliation is a crucial necessity in our complex, twenty-first-century world. How do we go about reconciling? I suggest that we need to move from one charcoal fire in John to another. After years of reading John's Gospel, I finally noticed these two fires. Maybe it is the Society of Jesus' recent call that we become "fires that kindle other fires" working on my imagination (General Congregation 35). Charcoal fires are transformative fires, rather than destructive blazes. In John 18:18, Peter is standing near a charcoal fire in the courtyard, and the maid, a gatekeeper, someone who lets in and keeps out, challenges him, "You are not one of this man's disciples, are you?" Peter replies with the first of the foretold damning denials: "I am not." His accent betrays him, as much as someone's accent from Montgomery, Alabama, would attract attention in Manhattan. Peter stands by the fire trying to get warm as the world grows cold preparing to crucify Jesus. Peter is hiding from his identity as a disciple of Jesus. He is trying to save his own butt. He is unable to accept the challenge of the cross. Peter's "I am not" stands in startling contradistinction to Jesus' proclamations of "I Am" throughout John's Gospel, "I Am" recalling God's words to Moses in Exodus 3:14, where God is revealed as "I Am Who I Am." Peter's "I am not" denies not only Jesus but also Peter's deepest truest self, which is rooted in his relationship with his friend and Lord, his savior and his God, Jesus, the one going to die for him and for us all.

Reconciliation moves us from the fire of comfort and safety to the fire of mission and transformation. John 21:9 is set in the glow of dawn's resurrection light as Jesus warms the hearts of his disciples, cooking fish and baking bread for them on the seaside charcoal fire. This fire fuels the disciples' courage. Such glowing Eucharist creates apostolic women like Mary Magdalene, and apostolic men like Peter and Paul, followers of Christ on mission to the world.

We need to be reconciled with God on personal and societal levels so we can become the healing presence of God in our world. The fire of God's love fans the flames of faith, making us desire to do in our times what the early disciples did in theirs; to do in our twenty-first century what St. Ignatius and St. Teresa of Avila did at the dawn of the modern age; to do what Pierre Teilhard de Chardin and Dorothy

Day and Martin Luther King did in the twentieth century. We want to be men and women on fire, radiating the transformative presence of the living God. Our prayer and sacraments make that presence tangible and real. Our service of others transforms those we serve and those of us who serve.

The twenty-first century may well be the time when we begin to take more seriously the trinitarian nature of our God. Many of us Catholics are, functionally, "Christo-monists." We pray to Jesus. We get in trouble and we beg Jesus to help us. Sometimes we call in God the Father. But we rarely beg the Holy Spirit to come to our aid. We converse more with Jesus than we do with the Spirit. The fires of Pentecost are looking for coals to light up. Our hearts and minds can be those coals when we open the depths of our being to God in prayer and engage the mysteries of the sacraments. The Holy Spirit can be as real to us as Jesus and set us aflame.

Alicia Keys sings, "Oh, she got both feet on the ground // And she's burning it down // Oh, she got her head in the clouds // And she's not backing down. // This girl is on fire // This girl is on fire // She's walking on fire //This girl is on fire." What would it be like if, twenty-five years from now, *Time* magazine (if there is a *Time* magazine twenty-five years from now) printed an article that described how the Catholic Church caught fire in 2013? With the new papacy of Pope Francis, some fires are definitely being lit. What would the authors describe as the ways in which the 1.2 to 1.3 billion Catholics became a global force for truth, justice, and freedom, so that "all people can be raised up to a new hope" (Eucharistic Prayer IV, "Jesus went about doing Good")?

One thing that would have to happen to see us become the red-hot glowing coals burning for God is a deep appreciation and knowledge of our faith. Too many of us know much more about our sports teams than we do about the fundamentals of Catholicism. I am constantly amazed that contestants on the TV quiz show *Jeopardy,* who know all kinds of arcane trivia from the history of the Ming Dynasty in the fourteenth century to who starred in some forgettable sitcom in 1971, don't know the simplest facts about Christianity or the Bible. The clue: a small village where Jesus turned water into wine. No one rings in. Another clue: Jesus compared the cares of our life to these kinds of flowers. Contestants guess: What are roses? What are marigolds? What are daffodils? Can anyone say, What are lilies of the field? (Matt 6:28). The Gospels are not obscure scholarly journals, but more and more of us know little of the basic facts of Jesus' life, death, and resurrection.

Years ago as a Jesuit novice, I was sent twice a week to teach catechism to a class of sixth graders. We got along, and the kids were well behaved and usually attentive, but there was this one little guy, call him Barney, who sat in the back, drew pictures, and spent the hour mostly looking out the window. He wasn't disrespectful or belligerent. He'd pay attention for a few minutes when I'd call him to realize he was in the room with us. But soon he'd be back in his own little world. One day I was babbling on about something and I said, ". . . and when Jesus comes back. . . ." Barney's head snapped up, his eyes got big, and he said in a loud voice, "He's coming back?" Astonishing news.

Yes, Jesus is coming back. He is already here and is directing all creation to fulfillment in the reign of God. We are agents of that re-creation of the universe. Our actions and choices have infinite value. The church is the mystical reality of Jesus' presence and future coming.

This book is a small attempt to help us know, and appropriate personally, the essentials of Catholic spirituality and practice. Our faith is a treasure worth sharing, a way of life worth living, a path of wisdom and transformation followed by billions who find themselves desiring a vibrant and real relationship with the living God. Here are the Top Ten basics you need to know in order to understand why it is Catholics believe what we believe and do what we do.

Again, the Indie Rock Group FUN has that great and haunting song, "Some Nights." It's a provocative and disturbing proclamation that many of our young people have no idea why we are alive or what we stand for: *"But I still wake up, I still see your ghost, Oh Lord, I'm still not sure what I stand for oh. Woah oh oh (What do I stand for?), Woah oh oh (What do I stand for?). Most nights I don't know anymore . . ."*

What do we stand for? What do we live for? For Catholics, it is these "Top Ten" essential realities of our faith. Living these truths will set us on fire and transform our world.

FR. RICK'S "TOP TEN" ESSENTIALS
OF CATHOLIC FAITH

"Of his own will he was born for us today, in time, so that he could lead us to his Father's eternity. God became man so that man might become God" (St. Augustine, *Sermo 13 de tempore,* in *Patrologia cursus completus, Series Latina,* ed. J.-P. Migne [Paris: 1844-64], vol. 39, cols. 1097-98; and Office of Readings, Saturday before Epiphany)

1. GOD LOVES US AND HAS CREATED US TO BE DIVINIZED (see 2 Peter 1:4 and *Catechism of the Catholic Church* §469: "For the Son of God became man so that we might become God"—St. Athanasius), to become human unto God as Jesus was ("so that God may be all in all" [1 Cor 15:28]). Human Persons, since we are made in the image of God, are persons, not things. A human person is someone, not something.

2. CREATION, AND ALL IN IT, IS GOOD, VERY GOOD, and must be utilized in order to help us reach our fulfillment. God wants all to receive salvation (1 Tim 2:4). God desires to communicate with us through creation and the realities and events of our lives.

3. JESUS THE ESSENTIAL GIFT: Jesus has shown us the way to God. What happened to Jesus happens to us. What we deeply and truly desire is to be with God forever, starting now.

4. CHRIST IS COMMUNITY: Jesus Christ is with us through our experience of community. His Mystical Body is the church, the people who form community in Christ's name and, as the pilgrim people of God, do in the world today what the Holy Spirit inspires us to do.

5. THE CHURCH, BOTH HUMAN AND DIVINE: That community, formed on the basis of tradition and Scripture, is ordered, organized. All the baptized have equal dignity. All have responsibility for forming and making the church effective and loving.   (*continued*)

6. RIGHTING RELATIONSHIPS: THE WORK OF JUS-TICE AND FORGIVENESS: The church responds to sin and suffering in the world, especially as it affects the poorest among us. Sin is that which violates creation and diminishes the love God wants all persons to experience. Sin is that which violates the human person. God's forgiveness reverses and restructures the effects of sin. Sin causes death. Forgiveness and grace foster life.

7. SACRAMENTS SING OUR STORIES: Through the sacraments, the church celebrates and challenges. "Sacraments are those signs that achieve in human hearts and lives what they signify to human minds" (Brian Daley, S.J.).

8. MISSION MATTERS: JESUS SAYS, "COME ON, WE'RE GOING TO CHANGE THE WORLD." The church is a church on mission. The question is not, "Does the church have a mission?" The question is, "Does the Mission have a church?" (Jon Sobrino, S.J.). The mission is the establishment of the kingdom of God in all realities, the realities, the letting God reign everywhere, in everyplace and in everyone. Let God be God. All the baptized are called to participate in Christ's mission.

9. PRACTICE MAKES US BETTER, NOT PERFECT: Through the practices of the Catholic way of life, we can live happy and healthy and holy and free, even in a world marred too often by sin and evil.

10. ☺☺☺ **SMILE: DESPITE IT ALL, THE UNIVERSE IS USER-FRIENDLY!** ☺☺☺ (see Isa 25:8; Rev 7:17; 21:4). "*Ama Deum et fac quod vis*" (Love and do what you will—St. Augustine, quoted in Lonergan 1972, 39).

". . . God, our savior, who desires everyone to be saved and to come to knowledge of the truth" (1 Tim 2:4).

". . . so that God may be all in all" (1 Cor 15:28).

Chapter 1

God Loves Us

*If you have never known the power of God's love, then maybe it
is because you have never asked to know it—I mean really asked,
expecting an answer.*

—Buechner, *Magnificent Defeat*, 35

*But, as it is written, "What no eye has seen, nor ear heard, nor
the human heart conceived, what God has prepared for those who
love him."*

—1 Corinthians 2:9

God loves us. Say it again. God loves us. It all begins and culmi-
nates with this seminal truth. God loves us. Any doctrine, idea,
way of being, church spokesperson that contradicts this reality isn't
Catholic, isn't loving, and isn't sane. God loves us. It sums up all the
teaching of Jesus, all the meanings of the sacraments, all the wisdom
of the church.

"This is my story, this is my song" goes the beautiful old hymn
"Blessed Assurance." This is our story, and this is our song, that God
is real and God loves us. Catholic Worker Jeff Dietrich says this isn't
just the greatest story ever told: "The Gospels are the greatest alternative story ever told" (Dietrich 2011, 13). According to Dietrich,
a tireless worker for peace and justice in Los Angeles, we need to
encounter the Gospels as an alternative to the stories that tell us the
pursuit of pleasure, profit, and power will make us whole and happy.
When we hear the Gospels as a freeing alternative, we find growing in

ourselves "a passionate desire to make the story real" (Dietrich 2011, 13). The great Jesuit apostle of social justice, Daniel Berrigan, writes, "All we have are these stories and each other" (quoted in Dietrich 2011, 11). The story begins, goes on, and ends with this deep truth: God loves us. The story of God as a fearsome bogeyman out to get us is not just false; it distorts the reality of love that undergirds our lives and the whole universe. God isn't out to "get us." God is here to love and transform us.

God loves us the way a good parent loves us. The way parents sacrifice for children never ceases to amaze me. In the latter days of August I am usually standing on the steps of some first-year students' dorm as Mom and Dad move their darling into digs decidedly less lavish than the home from which the student is moving. For many, a large room in a suburban East Coast home where they reigned as king or queen is traded for a small, cinder block domicile of sixty square feet that has to be shared with another person. Mom looks worried and excited both at the same time. Dad goes out to the truck or Suburban and gets the toolbox to make the room more amenable for the child they have nurtured and cared for 24/7 the past eighteen years. Joe or Jane looks bored or exasperated, both wanting Mom and Dad to leave and let them get on with the college adventure and also deeply wishing they could go back to being six years old and have the past twelve years to do all over again.

Too soon for the parents, the kid is left at the door. It is time for their child to enter adulthood and live on his or her own. Mom and Dad's anguish is as evident in the tears in their eyes and the catch in the throat. "Be good. Be safe. Have fun, but not too much fun. We'll call when we get home." Most likely there will be a call in an hour from the road.

For the first seven to ten days, the "first years" are ecstatic. Their roommate is universally "the most awesome kid I ever met." They love college and all that is new and enticing about being free from parental constraints. About day 10, all of a sudden, the whole first-year dorm, where I reside, is filled with kids who look like someone has just run over and killed their puppy. They are all missing Mom and

Dad. The roommate has started to get on their nerves. Every year in the first week or two, I make a point in homilies to address the reality of homesickness among the first years. It's sinking in that they just left the nicest place they will ever live, a home where you could eat the food and drive the car and not even be expected to contribute to the costs of groceries and gas. I tell them, "Of course you're homesick. Who wouldn't be? You mostly had wonderful parents. A great room. A dog. You even miss your little brother. Call your folks tonight and say thanks."

One family of four I know, not a rich family, but certainly not poor, spent $8,000 for a week at Disneyworld last year. At many universities, parents have to find somewhere between $25,000 and $50,000 annually so their son or daughter can get a college education. If you live in the Northeast of the United States and have a family income of $60,000 to $100,000 and hope to send your child to a private college, you can expect to pay somewhere near $384,150 in raising your child (www.babycenter.com). Where do parents find the generosity and sheer grit to marshal that kind of money? And where do they find the forgiveness and grace to lavish such largesse on someone who was a miserable teenager two short years before?

In the old TV series *The West Wing*, Toby Ziegler, the dour speech writer who never smiles, admits to Leo McGarry, President Bartlet's chief of staff, that he is fearful that he will not love his soon-to-be-born twins the way he has heard others speak of love for their children. Toby has heard that after the birth of a child all is different, nothing else matters, the child becomes the most important thing in life. Toby honestly realizes he has things he wants to do, and children may not fit into that schema. Later, the nurse presents him with two six pound three ounce beautiful, beanied babies, one in blue and the other in pink. He informs them their names are Molly and Huck, after his wife's father and a secret service agent who died in the line of duty. He tells them, "We're going to have to get you food and dentists and clothing. And whatever else you need. And no one told me you come with hats" (see Season 5, episode "The Dogs of War"). Toby is filled with an overwhelming love for his children. Toby gets it.

Most parents "get it" in one way or another. I have a friend whose teenage son wasn't doing very well in high school Spanish class. One Friday afternoon, my buddy picked up his son after school and asked how it was going with Spanish. "Just fine," the unloquacious son replied. Next week the report card came. His son had flunked Spanish. That evening the dad was yelling at his son, "I asked you just last Friday how you were doing in Spanish, and you said fine. And now your report card comes home telling me you flunked! Why'd you tell me you were doing fine?" The kid replied, "Dad, I only wanted to get yelled at once." My friend had to laugh. It's all about challenging his son while still loving his son no matter what. My friend gets it.

God gets it. God is like a good father. God is like a loving mother. In *Jesus of Nazareth*, Pope Benedict movingly reveals his view of God who exists like a parent in loving relationship.

> We see that to be God's child is not a matter of dependency, but rather of standing in the relation of love that sustains man's existence and gives it meaning and grandeur. One last question: Is God also Mother? The Bible does compare God's love with the love of a mother. . . . The mystery of God's maternal love is expressed with particular power in the Hebrew word *rahamim*, . . . 'womb,' later used to mean divine compassion, . . . God's mercy. The womb is the most concrete expression for the inter-relatedness of two lives and of loving concern. (Pope Benedict XVI 2007, 139)

God loves us desperately, totally, wholeheartedly. God created us and cares for us. God wants the best for us and for all the world. God gives us life, sustains us alive and promises us eternal life. God desires our salvation. God rejoices when we rejoice. God suffers when we suffer.

Bruce Lawrie offers one of the most moving testimonies to the love and care a father can have in his extraordinary essay about his severely mentally disabled six-year-old son, Matty. Lawrie's description of their bedtime routine moves to tears everyone to whom I've ever read it. God loves us the way Bruce loves his little boy, Matty.

> Matty holds his arm out in my direction, a tentative groping for me in the sudden blackness. I wrap his hand in mine and press

it to my face. I start singing the next song in our nightly rotation as I brush his hand against my whiskers, first his palm and then the back of his hand. He explores my face with his fingertips and then he covers my mouth gently. I sing into his palm, imagining the reverberations vibrating down into his little soul. How does he experience me? What am I in his world? I don't know. I may never know. . . .

I finish the song and stand up and wonder what heaven will be for my son. Maybe it'll be a place a lot like here, a place where his own son will run from him across a wide open field of green, every nerve-ending in his little body singing, where afterwards, Matty and I can tip back a beer together at a pub. Where he has a healthy body and a lovely wife and our family can linger long over pasta and homemade bread and salad and red wine. Where his son, my grandson, will fall asleep in my lap, a sweaty load of spent boy pinning me to my chair on the deck, the night sounds stirring around us, the stars rioting in the dark sky.

I look down on Matty's peaceful sleeping face. So often peace has eluded him: the operations, the I.V.s, the straps tying his hands to the hospital bed rails so he wouldn't pull the needles out, the countless blood draws when they couldn't find the vein, all the insults descending out of the blue onto my little boy who couldn't understand why the people around him had suddenly begun torturing him. But he is at peace right now. And a time is coming when he will have peace and have it to the full. And all the other things he's been robbed of. Meeting a girl. Playing catch with his father and his son. Making love. Calling his mother's name aloud. Talking with his twin sister. Eating a pizza. Drinking a beer. Running. And I'll get to be there with him. God will carve out a little slice of eternity for us, our own private do-over where the breeze carries the smell of fresh-cut grass, where the sky is bluer than you ever thought it could be, where the air feels newborn.

Soon, Matty. Soon. (Lawrie 2009).

A few days before Christmas a couple of years ago, a friend called and wanted to see me. He came into the office about 5:00 P.M. on a cold, dark December day. He was beyond distraught. His son was in prison. The son had a long history of drug problems. Once the son actually beat his father and stole the family car. Now he was calling, asking his father to bail him out. We talked and eventually discerned that maybe the best thing to do would be to leave the kid in prison. Let him realize that actions have consequences. The father, in his head, knew that would be the best choice in this situation. He wanted to do what his head was telling him to do, but his heart was tearing him up. "Father Rick, am I a terrible Dad for letting my boy stay in jail?" he asked in an anguished tone of voice that sounded like the Johnny Cash song "Hurt." I tried to affirm him in his decision. Oftentimes with addicts the best love is tough love. He left a little more accepting of what he had to do. Months later, it turns out the boy got out of prison and turned his life around. But with drugs and alcohol, all you can do is take life one day at a time. If that kid had died in prison, or gotten even more deeply mired in drugs, how would the father have felt? Would he be able to live with the consequences of choosing not to bail the kid out of jail? "Love is patient, Love is kind . . ." and love is demanding and difficult.

The most difficult thing I have done as a priest is to be present to parents who have lost their children. One family in Camden, New Jersey, lived through the pain and suffering of learning of the brutal rape and slaying of their thirteen-year-old daughter. It took over five years for dedicated law enforcement officials to find and bring the killer to justice. The girl's mother did not desire the death penalty for the murderer. But the man never apologized for what he did. That mother's face has always been for me the face of God. Even the look on a parent's face when informed their son has been killed in a car accident, or even the look on parents' faces when they show me pictures a totaled car from an accident their kids survived, gives some inkling of the depth and breadth of the way God feels about us. God loves us.

Many people have had trying, even horrendously painful, relationships with their biological parents. Not everyone's life has a Hollywood ending. Alcoholic parents can be beyond brutal, making family life a nightmare. Bipolar moms and dads can make childhood crushingly confusing. Many women share that their relationships with their own mothers are vexingly complex mixtures of like and dislike, love and almost hate. The mixed messages such parenting sends leave some of us reluctant to trust and unwilling and unable to love. The good news is that God is not your father or my father, as good or bad as those human men might have been. God is Our Father. The mystery God is, actually, is communicated to us by this image of a good and loving Father. Jesus called God "Abba," the Aramaic word for "Daddy."

Parents have a fierce and formidable love for their children. Maybe it was the fact that priests and bishops have no children that caused such cluelessness to criminality when celibates were called to respond to the crisis of child sex abuse by priests. Many bishops and religious superiors didn't get it. For a parent, the most important person in the world is one's child. That's how God feels about us. We are the most precious part of creation. St. Ignatius's *Spiritual Exercises* begin with the Principle and Foundations that all things have been created for us, and we are to use all things to attain the goal of our existence, that is, eternal union in love with our loving God.

None of us can cause ourselves to exist. None of us can live without something beyond us causing and sustaining our existence. God, like a good parent, is the underlying reality that makes us what we are and gives us all we have. We are created by God to love and be in relationship with God through this life and be transformed into those who can live with God forever.

Can this really be true? Is it possible that the all-encompassing power that creates and sustains us and our world with its seven billion plus people, our universe with its billions of galaxies, really cares for and loves us, really knows and cares about and loves me?

Cardinal Francis Eugene George of Chicago tells the story of a visit to Africa. Some men came from a small village to visit the church. They had heard of the stories about Jesus. They wanted to talk to the local priest to learn more about our faith and went to the door of the small house next to the church. One man stayed outside as his friends entered, and Cardinal George struck up a conversation with him. When Cardinal George asked him why he didn't go in to listen to the priest as his friends had done, the man replied, "Oh, I've thought about what we've heard, even while I was walking here, and I've decided that it makes no sense when I look at my life—that God would love us, that God would sacrifice himself for us, that God is stronger than the spirits that harm us. I don't believe it. It's too good to be true" (George 2009, 260).

Isn't it too good to be true? Isn't this all just wishful thinking, the Freudian creating of an imaginary friend, a fairy-tale parent/friend, who makes up for the crushing pulverizing pain of human life? Come on. It's a world that science has shown to be a red-clawed reality, where the strong eat the weak, and we suffer and subsist our seventy or eighty years before being obliterated into nothingness.

Do you believe that bleak vision of the meaning of our existence? The best argument for life after life isn't Dr. Eben Alexander's *Proof of Heaven* and others' near-death experiences. The best proof of life after life is the fact we are alive now. Why would whatever, or better said, whoever, brings us into existence, stop causing us to exist when our bodies no longer function? Our bodies are constantly changing. In a real sense, we are constantly dying. "Life is a disease and the prognosis is death" goes the old joke. You can believe that life is a miraculous gift and hope for that gift to be continued beyond the grave, or you can believe that life is a meaningless surd, that we are here for a while and then, poof, we're gone. Our lives mean nothing and our existence has no purpose. Or you can struggle to believe that the evidence of our being here now intimates something transcendental. Our lives give witness to the fact that our creator loves us and has great dreams for the meaning of our existence.

Why would you choose meaninglessness over meaning? Because meaning cannot be scientifically proven? But science cannot prove the meaning of anything. Science is a powerful and wonderful way of knowing, and can reveal much of beauty and wonder. Still science can only tell us what something is and how it works. Science cannot tell us why something exists and for what it exists.

Even scientists have firm faith. They believe in the scientific method. They believe that the simpler explanation of phenomena trumps more complicated theories, that is, Occam's Razor. They believe that only that which is falsifiable is real. They believe that what is replicable is more true than an experiment or experience that cannot be duplicated. They believe that what is more beautiful and symmetrical will more likely lead to the development of the correct theory. As Jesuit Brother Guy Consolmagno says about his scientific work as an astronomer for the Vatican Observatory, "If I never had believed it, I never would have seen it." Physicists looking for dark matter or the elusive, tiny, vibrating strings of string theory believe that those things might be there before they actually discover such realities.

Faith is a gift given us. Faith is "the assurance of things hoped for, the conviction of things unseen" (Heb 11:1). We believe that God became what we are so we can become what God is. That's not some Jesuit's wild twist on theology. That's St. Athanasius in the third century (CCC §460). This has been the faith of the church long before Jesuit Karl Rahner began explaining it in dense prose in the twentieth century.

God creates us as persons, not things. Jesuit mystic and scientist Pierre Teilhard de Chardin cogently notes, "We are not human beings having a spiritual experience. We are spiritual beings having a human experience" (Teilhard de Chardin 2002). We have the powers of understanding, choosing, and loving. God cannot force us to love. God cannot make us love ourselves, others, or even God. We have to make sense of our lives and our existence. The only way we can ultimately make sense of the whole of our lives is to have faith. It begins with the simple trust in our own powers of consciousness. I am certain I exist. There was a Jesuit who was on the witness stand once after witnessing a crime and the defense lawyer was hammering away at his testimony. "Are you certain you saw this? Are you certain you saw that?" After a while, the Jesuit replied, "Look buddy, I teach philosophy. Some days, I'm only 50 percent certain I exist."

Most of us don't suffer the philosopher's malaise. We know we are here. We know we are the person we were yesterday. None of us really think we are living a dream. We know. We know that we know. To say I don't know would mean that I, at least, know that—that I don't know. Therefore to claim one doesn't know is self-refuting. Even to say you don't know proves you're a knower.

As knowers we choose on the basis of what and whom we know. The vast majority of what we know is based on what we take on faith from the testimony of others. I've never been to China, but I'm sure it's there. I cannot sequence my DNA but I firmly accept that I have this blueprint of life in every one of the trillions of cells that make up my body.

I am also sure that I love some persons, that I am friends with many other persons, and that I am merely acquainted with and care for multiple others. There are billions on this earth whom I do not know and who do not know me, but I trust and believe they are persons just like you and me. When a newborn child miraculously emerges from a woman, the child's parents love that child as fiercely and fervently as Toby Ziegler loved his twins. We all need food and shelter, but also loving relationships and a meaning for living.

The Catholic way of life is a blueprint for living. The practices of Catholicism, our sacraments, our prayer, our service of others, especially the poor and marginalized, show us how to be persons in relation with one another. We hope and trust in persons. We know that the justice and peace we want for our children are the justice and peace all people want for their children. Our God who loves us the way parents love children, calls us to love all peoples as our brothers and sisters. This is the great revolution of Jesus' Beatitudes. This is the way we change the world in light of the vision of Matthew 25. This is codified and explicated in the centuries-long tradition of Catholic social teaching.

We Catholics, like those of other faith traditions and those of good will, want a world of love and justice and peace. We need to know how to construct societies and cultures that sustain and foster life and love, and we need the courage and hope to choose such ways of relating to one another. Such is the work of love. As God loves us, so we are to love one another. We are to parent and care for one another as sisters and brothers united in love.

It's all so simple to articulate and describe. It is all so difficult to live out. And despite all the trials and tragedies of human life, despite the Hitlers and cancers and wars and tsunamis, we are given the grace, the power, to believe. St. Thomas Aquinas taught that grace is the ability to do what you could not do before (Connor 2006, 263). Let us pray for the grace to believe. Let's choose to trust. Let's allow ourselves to know God's love and live out of the reality of that relationship.

How did I come to believe this? How did I come to know God loves us? I entered the Society of Jesus in Wernersville, Pennsylvania in 1976. After ten days or so, we Jesuit novices made a three-day silent retreat. On the first evening of the retreat, George Aschenbrenner, the novice director, gave a short talk, orienting us to the retreat and beginning the school of prayer that the two-year novitiate is, among other things. That talk changed my life. Somewhere in that little "points for prayer" talk, George just simply said, "God loves you." I don't know why, and I can't explain it. But the truth of those three little words hit me like a ton of bricks. I was completely captivated and made aware of God's love for me. I had heard that God loved me, I guess, somewhere in my Catholic childhood, but I had been far away from the church in my wild adolescent and college years. I obviously had thought a lot about God in the year before joining the Jesuits. Still, for three days I walked in a cloud of awareness that something radical had changed in my soul. I knew God loved me and could never again doubt or deny the experience. God's love struck me dumb. I was silent for three days, but really had no desire to speak (and it wasn't all that difficult. We were all on silence anyway). I just was aware of God, and God's mysterious connection to me, personally. I knew God's love and wanted to learn how to respond.

I was lucky. I hadn't done anything to earn God's love. I certainly didn't know how important a grace realization of God's love is for one who wanted to become a Jesuit. It just happened. I hope it can happen to you. Just pray and ask God to let you know and experience God's love for you.

The more I've grown in a deepening appreciation of God's love for me and all humanity, the more I've come to trust in that experience of the first days of my life as a novice. God's love undergirds my daily existence, is the North Star of my choices (on my better days), and is the defining reality and meaning of my life. God's love calls me, and calls us all, to love one another. We are all created by God to love God by loving one another.

The great bishop and martyr Óscar Romero said,

> You and I and all of us are worth very much, because we are creatures of God, and God has prodigially [*sic*] given his wonderful gifts to every person. And so the church values human beings and contends for their rights, for their freedom, for their dignity. . . . The church values human beings and cannot tolerate that an image of God is trampled by persons that become brutalized by trampling on others. (Romero 1998, 6)

Even those who have been trampled on can sometimes be the most poignant and powerful preachers of a God who loves. Given all the pain, humiliation, and suffering even highly celebrated African Americans endured under twentieth-century Jim Crow laws and the hundreds of years of slavery before, how does a Louis Armstrong sing the greatest song ever written? Maybe he knows God's love and communicates that love to the world.

What a Wonderful World

I see trees of green, red roses too
I see 'em bloom, for me and for you
And I think to myself, what a wonderful world.
I see skies of blue, clouds of white
Bright blessed days, dark sacred nights
And I think to myself, what a wonderful world.
The colors of a rainbow, so pretty in the sky

Are also on the faces, of people going by.
I see friends shaking hands, sayin' how do you do
They're really sayin', I love you.
I hear babies cry, I watch them grow
They'll learn much more, than I'll never know
And I think to myself, what a wonderful world.

CHAPTER 2

Creation, and All in It, Is Good, Very Good

We are losing the attitude of wonder, contemplation, listening to creation. The implications of living in a horizontal manner [is that] we have moved away from God, we no longer read His signs.
—Pope Francis, Audience in Rome, June 5, 2013

The way humanity treats the environment influences the way it treats itself, and vice versa. . . . The Church has a responsibility towards creation and she must assert this responsibility in the public sphere. In so doing, she must defend not only earth, water and air as gifts of creation that belong to everyone. She must above all protect mankind from self-destruction. . . . Just as human virtues are interrelated, such that the weakening of one places others at risk, so the ecological system is based on respect for a plan that affects both the health of society and its good relationship with nature.
—Pope Benedict XVI, *Caritas in Veritate* §51

After three years of studying for the master of divinity degree ("Stalking and bagging the coveted M.Div." the joke went among us Jesuit scholastics), we had to take comprehensive exams. The test basically covered the major areas of theological studies—ecclesiology, revelation, sacraments, biblical theology, and so on. The examiners could ask us anything, which meant that the test basically covered all of theology, a huge amount of intellectual material. I remember the look I got when I told the three examiners in the two-hour oral exam, "It's all creation and eschatology. Everything else is just filler."

What I was getting at is the truth that creation implies a creator, and the creator desires something of and for creation. What God wants for creation is that all creatures reach their culmination, the end for which they are created. God wants everything to be fulfilled. God "desires everyone to be saved" (1 Tim 2:4). When everything reaches the fulfillment for which God made all that is, God will be "all in all" (1 Cor 15:28).

God loves us, and all of creation exists to help us achieve the goal for which we are created: eternal life with God forever. Think about this a bit. Everything is good. Our planet, our bodies, our social systems—all is gift, all is grace. We need to use things in ways that establish right relationships, that is, justice.

How do we know God? A friend of mine, a reflective, iconoclastically spiritual Irish American East Coast lawyer, read a book about dialogues with God and was awed by the idea that God is always communicating with us. In telling me about the book, he exuberantly and loudly argued, "God is shouting, all the time. The problem is we aren't listening. We aren't paying attention."

The primordial way God speaks to us is through creation. Once at Holy Name parish in Camden, New Jersey, we were having evening workshops on the Bible. Most of the people had put in a full day's work, many of them physically demanding jobs in factories or as nurses' aides in hospitals. We would gather about seven in the evening and have a short talk and then quickly get into small groups in order to allow people to start talking and not fall asleep as the Jesuit droned on about scripture. This one evening we were talking about Moses and the burning bush and how God had spoken to Moses through this experience. One woman in the group shared how she felt that she had never really had an experience of God. I gently asked, "What about when your kids were born?" She replied, "Oh, that's what we mean by an experience of God? Wow. That's right. I never felt closer to God than when I was giving birth." And after a pregnant pause she added, "Gee. Talk about a burning bush. . . ." The whole group erupted in laughter at her earthy joke. But all of us understood what she was saying. We experience God in the deepest and most transcendental moments of our lives.

We also can be aware of and know God in the daily grind of our existence. If we're lucky and live eighty years, we have some 29,200 days on earth. In every minute of every hour God is there with us, as close as our own heartbeat. God is as close and real to us as every breath we take. We never experience God directly. God is mystery. God is always so much greater than we, as human beings, can comprehend or experience. In some ways when dealing with God we are like dogs staring at the computer screen. We are on a different level from God. We are limited creatures, created to exist in certain times and spaces. God is omnipresent and eternal. God wants to bring us through this created existence to union with God in the next life. This process of divinization doesn't start when we die. It starts when we are conceived and is sacramentally inaugurated when we are baptized. All of life is speaking to us of the mysterious, often unnamed and unthematized presence of the mystery of God. But rare is the person who sees a magnificent sunset and just shrugs their shoulders and walks away. At the start of Pat Conroy's magnificent novel *The Prince of Tides*, a mother takes her small children out to the dock to watch the sunset. As the fire-red glowing orb disappears beneath the horizon, her small child exclaims, "Please Momma, do it again." Prayer is our effort to witness God doing it again and again and again.

One way we become more aware of God and God's constant divinizing presence is through the practice of prayer. The comedian Lilly Tomlin once joked, "How come when we talk to God, it's called prayer, but when God talks to us, it's schizophrenia?"

Prayer is a risk. When I was a Jesuit novice, I remember a community meeting during which someone asked our provincial, Fr. Al Panuska, S.J., about the biggest problem he faced. His blunt and honest answer startled me: "Jesuits not praying." As novices, our lives were structured in such a way that not praying was impossible. Still, once out of the structured life of the novitiate, I have learned, painfully at times, that the demands of the apostolic works can too easily crowd out the time set aside for prayer (although I always seem to find the ten minutes to catch Jay Leno's monologue . . .). Why is it so difficult to engage in the demanding practice of deep and transformative contemplative prayer?

What is prayer? We know that many people pray, that prayer is something we as Catholic Christians ought to do, and we hear that prayer can change things. But many of us feel conflicted and confused when we go to pray. Does God really respond to our prayers? Does God really listen to, or care about, what we say? If we prayed some other way, or prayed more regularly and faithfully, would we be better people? Can our praying make the world a better place? In our age, which tends to elevate activism to ethereal heights, wouldn't our time be better spent serving the poor, or doing something for somebody in need? Wouldn't God be interested more in our doing something "worthwhile" than in our sitting in silence, trying not to pay attention to the random thoughts rumbling endlessly around in our heads? And when we get right down to it, don't we all sometimes ask ourselves, Does prayer really work? Does prayer really do anything?

The way to move forward and avoid getting stuck in the spiritual whirlpool such questions generate is to realize that prayer is a risk. There is no science of prayer. Just as you cannot prove scientifically the worth or effects of real love, the day-in and day-out loving and caring and living with other persons, you cannot prove the worth of prayer, the day-in and day-out practice of paying attention to God. If we could scientifically prove prayer's value, it wouldn't be prayer. Prayer is a risk because prayer is a lifelong, life-changing, act of faith. The word "believe" comes from the German *belieben*, meaning "to belove." Prayer is all about the risks involved in loving.

Much of our reluctance and resistance to risk prayer is rooted in our fear of God's really responding to us. On the one hand, we fear that God won't take us seriously. On the other hand, we are quite afraid that God will take us very seriously, as seriously as we take ourselves, and our loved ones. Prayer is a risk because the God who calls us to conversion and transformation takes us up on the invitation to get involved in our lives. And when that happens, the adventure begins.

Being on fire, living as Catholics, makes us realize that we and God are involved in amazing transformations. Human being is all about our being changed into people who can become one with God and exist with God forever. We are offered the opportunity to "come to share in the divine nature" (2 Pet 1:4 *New American Bible*). All of us, all of the cosmos, are in the processes of radical transformation (Rom 8:21). The present yet ever coming kingdom of God will be established fully, and God will be "all in all" (1 Cor 15:28). *Lumen Gentium*, the great document of Vatican II that describes what the church is and ought to be, tells what Catholicism is all about. God desires "to dignify men and women with a participation in His own divine life" (*Lumen Gentium* §2). I'm not saying this because I'm some kind of "radical," "unorthodox," "off the reservation" Jesuit who drinks the Karl Rahner Kool-Aid. In the fourth century St. Athanasius said, "the Son of God became Man so that we might become God" (CCC §460). Prayer makes us pay more attention to, and commit ourselves to realizing, our transformation in Christ. It's a risk to trust God. It's a risk to refuse to cooperate in the transformations God offers us. But it's a better bet to freely accept who God is and what God is making of our lives.

Prayer is relational. All prayer is relational. By praying, we relate to God, our God who loves us passionately, consistently, challengingly. When we truly relate to one we love, especially when that one is Jesus, we may be called to change. The parent who loves a child suffering from cystic fibrosis changes in many ways. The son or daughter loving an aging mother or father makes many unexpected life changes. Such changes always call us to deeper, more active love. Knowing that extreme poverty can be alleviated across the globe changes one who prays about it. Witness U2's lead singer Bono and the ONE campaign to eradicate extreme poverty (www.one.org). When we pray, we risk changing and being changed. Prayer may make us know that we need to change. Prayer may make us able to change things, from addictions to unhealthy relationships to social problems. Prayer may make us willing and able to do for God and for others something we never imagined doing. Prayer will makes us into saints.

Prayer is relational because we relate to God on both personal and communal levels of reality. We never pray alone. Always, and in all ways, you/we and someone else are praying. As soon as we try to pray, God takes us up on the offer. Prayer is not a competition, or a "goal"-oriented activity. To pray is to already have "won." Prayer is much more like making love, or hitting a baseball, or learning to play a musical instrument (sometimes loudly and badly!), than it is like getting a promotion, or achieving a goal, or mastering a skill. Prayer is more like floating on water than paddling stridently to get somewhere. Prayer is more "Letting Go" than "Holding On." Prayer is a journey wherein we're simply "being there" while somewhat paradoxically always being "on the road." Prayer is allowing our lives to be harmonized. Prayer is getting our lives and loves in order, and prayer is inviting God's ordering of our loves and lives.

We are all being divinized. Pray-ers know this truth. To be aware of, and cooperate with, divinization takes work. Real prayer is work, that is, disciplined spirituality, as is Catholicism. We need to recognize that consolation is not always comfortable, and desolation is not always disagreeable. Pat O'Sullivan, an Australian Jesuit, once told Jesuits in formation, "The sailors going to the whorehouse may seem happy, but they are not in consolation." St. Ignatius teaches us that prayer is the dedicated monitoring of consolation and desolation in our experience. We go with the consolations of life that communicate God's presence, and we struggle against the desolations that separate us from our sense of God's presence.

Being disciplined about prayer is essential if we want to see the benefits of prayer, just as regular physical exercise is necessary to get and keep our bodies in shape. The more in shape we are spiritually, the more we are likely to realize and recognize God in our lives. Prayer is the effort to consciously experience God. Praying is consciously paying attention to the central relationships of our lives, our relationship with ourselves, with others, and with God. Our relationship with God is the one that makes all these other relationships possible. Prayer is focusing conscious attention on our relationship with God and finding the whispers of God's presence in the relationships of our lives. We speak to God in prayer and the word God speaks back is our life.

Prayer is paying attention to what is really real. Prayer isn't just finding God in all things. It's more than that. Prayer is seeking God in all realities, realities that were, are, and are to come. The awareness of God and the processes of divinization in our hearts and minds is evident in how we make choices.

On a moral level, prayer leads us to wisdom and correct choosing. When I was a little kid, in wintertime, my mother used to dress us up in those bulky, blue snowsuits that made us look like midget Michelin men. She would let me and my brother out along with the dog. As soon as I ran out to play in the white winter wonderland, I'd reach down and grab a mitten full of the cold, delicious snow and begin to eat. My mom would yell from the kitchen door, "Ricky, don't eat the yellow snow!" Prayer is learning what is and is not "yellow snow." What is not good for us is whatever frustrates and foils our transformation in Christ. For serious pray-ers, life becomes a series of exercises wherein we discern what we truly and deeply desire. Such holy desires reveal God's will for us, and prayer mediates the grace that helps us choose what we deeply desire and thus make the right choices.

Prayer, practiced regularly and faithfully, can become a centering fulcrum of our daily lives, keeping us on plan and focused. Prayer even engaged in sporadically and frenetically is valuable. Anne Lamott, one of the most refreshing, if iconoclastic, contemporary writers on prayer, says the two best prayers are "Thank You" and "Help." She recently added, "Wow!"

How to Pray? Prayer doesn't have to be elaborate to function as a current carrying us through life to life eternal. There are many methods of praying: prayers of petition (probably the most common form of prayer), daily Mass, the Liturgy of the Hours; daily spiritual reading; systematically and slowly working one's way through various books of the Bible; taking some time during the week to read through the readings for the upcoming Sunday; the Rosary; eucharistic adoration; the utterly simple but demanding practice of Centering Prayer. These are all valid methods of praying. Prayer groups are helpful for many people. The main thing is to choose freely a method you find agreeable. No one stays with a prayer practice they find tedious and frustrating. Experiment with unconventional methods that utilize and stimulate the imagination: See a movie with Jesus; write someone a letter while in prayer mode; create a dialogue with the Holy Spirit; draw pictures for God. The imagination is the arena wherein we can often most powerfully experience God. Ignatian contemplation of Gospel scenes is a tried and true example of using our graced imagination in prayer.

There are good prayer guides. Many have traversed the paths through the forest of prayer. Don't feel you have to reinvent the wheel. For the beginner, Jesuit Mark Thibodeaux's *Armchair Mystic* is a great starter book. Pushing Jesuit works on prayer may seem too much like I'm pushing the family business, but anyone who knows about free and freeing spirituality will agree that anything by Tony De Mello, S.J., is worth reading and pondering. Franciscan Richard Rohr's amazingly brief and deceptively simple *Everything Belongs* is the best book I've ever read on prayer. Rohr orients the twenty-first-century person to what prayer is and can be. *The Cloud of Unknowing* is a classic book on prayer and is the inspiration for the contemporary Trappist method of Centering Prayer. Anne Lamott's *Traveling Mercies, Plan B*, and *Help, Thanks, Wow: The Three Essential Prayers*, are wild zany takes on everything from prayer to writing to parenting to eating disorders. Ernest Kurtz and Katherine Ketchem's *The Spirituality of Imperfection* is a real jewel. There are many more good books one can read. Magazines like *America, U.S. Catholic, St. Anthony's Messenger,* and *Commonweal* are excellent sources and guides for spiritual reading. The Internet, where so many young adults spend their reading time, offers great sites like the Irish Jesuits' "Sacred Space" (http://www.sacredspace.ie) to orient one to prayer. Jesuit Creighton University offers a wealth of material (http://onlineministries. creighton.edu/CollaborativeMinistry/online.html).

What does prayer do? Ultimately the practice of real and consistent prayer changes our desires. When we find ourselves wanting what God wants we are in right relationship with God, and that is the experience of justice on the personal level. Prayer practiced over time will lead us through the processes that the *Spiritual Exercises* of St. Ignatius aim to elicit: prayer will free us from, free us for, and free us to be with. Free from all that frustrates our transformation in Christ, from addictions to personality faults. Free for service and the righting of relationships on many levels, which ultimately is the work of constructing social justice for all. Free to be with God as the Holy Spirit works our transformation in Christ, thus actualizing our freely being our deepest, truest selves in relation with others. Real prayer is much more about deep transformation and everyday mysticism than it is about magic and cheap grace.

Prayer doesn't do anything if we don't pray. I go to the gym three times a week, once a year. The results, or lack thereof, are rather predictable. Regular, consistent, committed prayer is worth the effort, but we'll never know it until we do it. Go ahead. Take the risk. Then we can authentically urge others to follow our example. St. Ignatius once said, "There are very few men who realize what God would make of them if they abandoned themselves entirely to His hands, and let themselves be formed by His Grace" (to Ascanio Colonna, Rome, April 25, 1543).

Prayer done with an open heart and mind will most likely bring us to a deep and awestruck appreciation for creation and the incredible universe of which we are a part. The revelations of science in the past few centuries have been startlingly stunning. Billions of galaxies and 13.7 billion years of evolution bring us an astonishingly deeper and richer awareness of how awesome our creator is.

A few years ago, I got a great deal on a box gift set of hardback copies of Stephen Hawking's *A Brief History of Time* and *The Universe in a Nutshell* on the Borders bookstore's five-dollar table. I couldn't believe my luck, getting those books at that price, and having tried the *Brief History* once before, I found the version with pictures to be quite helpful. As I was working my way through *The Universe in a Nutshell*, the following sentence leapt off the page: "The idea that the universe has multiple histories may sound like science fiction, but is now accepted as science fact" (Hawking 2001, 80). Multiple histories? How did I miss that memo? This means that there is not just one history, but that every possible history happens. In the many-histories, many-universes view of contemporary physics, everything is not just possible; everything happens. In this history or universe, I am Fr. Rick, the Jesuit. In another, I'm a fireman, what I wanted to be when I was seven, like my godfather Uncle Richie. In another, I die in the Vietnam War. In still another, I'm a Philadelphia Eagles linebacker.

Our commonsense world is not the "real" world that determines our lives and futures. Actually, our world(s) are only one of many in the universe(s). Some physicists claim that the multiverse is an established fact. In reading Stephen Hawking, Brian Greene, and others, I came to new realizations about the ways in which physics has completely reordered the facts about physical reality. These findings have huge implications for our understandings of God, the future (and the past), and what heaven and eternal life are like. How we imagine our physical reality is a prime constituent of how we understand the God to whom we pray and the efficacy of the prayers we make. In order to comprehend our faith, we must take into account what scientists are discovering.

The discoveries of physicists in the past century have been radically revolutionary. Since Einstein took us beyond Newton's equations, revealing the centrality of the speed of light as an absolute by which we could measure the realities of matter and energy ($E = mc^2$), we have never been able to sense the world in quite the same, limited manner we did previously. In 1927, Msgr. Georges Lemaitre, a Catholic priest from Belgium, applied Einstein's theories to the questions of cosmology and began to develop the "Big Bang" theory. He hypothesized that the universe began as an incredibly powerful explosion from an almost unimaginable dense singularity smaller than the size of a pinhead. Lemaitre stridently cautioned that he was doing physics, and that his theory was not designed to justify the creation account found in Genesis. George Gamow and others worked out the details of Lemaitre's discoveries. Edwin Hubble discovered the "redshift" of galaxies (a measure of the distance of other galaxies from our own Milky Way) and thus demonstrated that the universe is expanding. Fritz Zwicky discovered "dark matter." Some 95 percent of the universe is made up of dark matter or dark energy, while only 5 percent is what we think of as ordinary "matter" (Cannato 2006, 32). In 1998, Saul Perlmutter and Robert Kirshner stunned us all by showing that the universe isn't just expanding; it's doing so at an accelerating rate. In a *New York Times* op-ed, Brian Greene wonders what will happen in the distant future when all the other stars and planets are so far from Earth that they will not be visible to our eyes or to our instruments. People at that time will have to accept on faith and from the testimony of our times that there is really something "out there" (Greene 2011).

We now know that we live in a vast, pulsating universe, filled with trillions of stars and billions of galaxies. Our investigation and understanding of scientific theories concerning the expanding (and accelerating) universe, black holes, dark matter, dark energy, string theory, and the multiverse, radically reorient our comprehension of the majesty and mystery of the universe(s) and thus our awareness of the awesomeness of God.

Scientists agree on these facts. The Big Bang occurred some 13.7 billion years ago, and 4.6 billion years ago the solar system formed. The moon is 240,000 miles from earth. The sun is 93 million miles away. Light travels 186,281 miles per second and a light year is the distance light travels in a year. The Milky Way is so big that light traveling at light speed (186,000 miles per second; 6 trillion miles per year) takes 100,000 years to leap from rim to rim. The Milky Way spans 100,000 light years! At light speed, the Andromeda galaxy, our closest neighbor, is 4.6 million light years away. The closest star to us is 26 trillion miles away. The stars within 220 light years of the sun encompass only 1 part in 10 million of the total number of stars in our Milky Way galaxy, which consists of some 300 to 400 billion stars. There are more than 100 billion galaxies in the known universe (see Goldsmith 1991; Morris 1990).

Many have compared all of cosmic time to one year. Doing so means that the advent of *Homo sapiens* happens around 7:30 A.M., December 31, and all of recorded history happens in the final minute of the year.

Cosmic Timeline

Millions of Years Ago	Event	Date
13,700	BIG BANG	Jan. 1
4,600	Milky Way galaxy forms	Mar. 1
3,800	Oldest known rocks form	Mar. 5
3,600	Oldest known fossils	Mar. 21
2,000 (approx.)	Significant oxygen in atmosphere	July 26
650 (approx.)	Multi-celled life in oceans	Nov. 10
590	Fossil record begins	Nov. 14
440	Life moves to land	Nov. 25
400	Fish (vertebrates) abound	Nov. 29
250	Dinosaurs appear	Dec. 12
65	Dinosaurs disappear	Dec. 26

******* December 31 ********

4.0	First Hominids	7:30:00 AM
1.6	Hominids	1:30:00 PM
	First Humans	10:30:00 PM
	Widespread use of stone tools	11:00:00 PM
	Domestication of fire in China	11:46:00 PM
0.4 - 0.1	First Homo Sapiens	11:49:00 PM
	Begin most recent glacial era	11:56:00 PM

(continued)

	Extensive cave paintings in Europe	11:59:00 PM
0.8	Agriculture	11:59:20 PM
	First cities	11:59:35 PM
0.005	Recorded history	11:59:34 PM
	Renaissance in Europe	11:59:59 PM

******* ALL IN THE LAST 10 MINUTES OF Dec. 31 ********

500,000	Rapid Brain Expansion
400,000	HOMO SAPIENS
250,000	Fire in use / Pre-modern speech
150,000-60,000	Neanderthals (?)
35,000-30,000	Homo Sapiens Sapiens (full brain and speech)
20,000-15,000	Religious ritual and cave painting
11,000- 8,000	Agriculture
6,000	Cities
250	Industrial revolution

(see Sagan 1977, 14-15; Coyne 2005)

Further investigation reveals a curious revelation. The universe seems to be made in a way that is incredibly and marvelously trimmed and tuned. If the Big Bang had been an iota of a fraction stronger, nothing would have formed. If the Big Bang had been a fraction of an iota weaker, gravity would have collapsed, pulling everything back into a black hole or singularity. If creation were not so finely tuned, on many levels, and in innumerable arenas, we would not be here. "It appears, therefore, that we exist in a very improbable kind of universe, one that was fine-tuned to an accuracy of one part in 10^{15} at a time of one second after the big bang. In fact, this fine-tuning was even greater at earlier times. At some point, when the universe was only a fraction of a second old, it would have been not one part in 10^{15}, but one part in 10^{50}" (Morris 1990, 53). With just very excruciatingly infinitesimal minor changes in creation, human persons would never have evolved, nor survived (see Morris 1990, 211ff.).

In his fascinating *New Proofs for the Existence of God*, Jesuit Robert Spitzer argues that the fact of the "extreme improbability" of our universe producing humans like us "begs for an explanation beyond mere 'chance occurrence'" (Spitzer 2010, 67). Spitzer quotes Fred Hoyle: "A common sense interpretation of the facts suggests that a superhuman intellect has monkeyed with physics, as well as with chemistry and biology, and that there are no blind forces worth speaking about in nature" (Spitzer 2010, 73).

We exist. We are here-and-now, whatever "here" and "now" ultimately mean. Life is a gift, and gifts imply givers. Let us praise the giver. *Deo Gratias.*

Prayer on creation also makes us realize how short and fragile our time is on this earth. Eighty years is some 29,200 days. That's 4,160 weeks. Life goes quickly. Ten years is 520 more Saturdays. By then, I'll be sixty-seven years old. No one ever told their doctor on a diagnosis of cancer, "Wow, Doc. I wish I'd worked more weekends." Make life count. It is precious and short.

We also live at a time when concerns about life on this planet are deepening and growing. Climate change and the warming of the atmosphere portend incredible changes in the next century. Ethical questions surrounding energy production and consumption proliferate. Pollution from over seven billion people poses more than a challenge: it is a question of survival. Will we be the ones who save or destroy life on this pale, blue dot on the edge of the Milky Way galaxy? That is as much a theological as a scientific question.

Our God is a God of tremendous changes and transformations. We prayerfully learn this by attending to the stories of salvation history, by listening carefully to the ever-changing desires of our hearts through our lifetimes, and by marveling at the revelations of science in our times. Noted scientist and theologian Franciscan Sr. Ilia Delio (she has two Ph.D. degrees! When do people like her sleep?) sculpts challenging theological works integrating the insights and implications of the meanings of an evolutionary universe for our faith and for our lives.

> Change is integral to God because God is love and love is dynamic relatedness. God is eternally becoming ever newness in love and God's ever newness in love is the inner source

of evolution toward newness and greater union in love. . . . The emergence of Christ depends on our capacity to love, to become whole-makers. The love of God is poured out into our hearts through the Holy Spirit, and is always new. . . . The God of evolution is the God of adventure, a God who loves to do new things and is always new. We are invited into this adventure of love to find our freedom in love and to love without measure. (Delio 2011, 153, 156)

Chapter 3

Jesus: The Essential Gift

A mother was making pancakes one Saturday morning for her two little boys. The brothers began squabbling over who was going to get the first pancake. Mom, as mothers often do, saw an opportunity to teach her little boys a lesson. "You know, if Jesus was here he'd say 'My brother can have the first pancake.'" So the five year old turns to the three year old and says, "OK. You be Jesus."

. . . the most important thing we can do is not worship Jesus, but listen to him. Listening is the central motif of the Gospel.
—Dietrich, *Broken and Shared*, 295

Look, whatever thoughts you have about God, who He is or if He exists, most will agree that if there is a God, He has a special place for the poor. In fact, the poor are where God lives. . . . the one thing we can all agree, all faiths and ideologies, is that God is with the vulnerable and poor. God is in the slums, in the cardboard boxes where the poor play house. God is in the silence of a mother who has infected her child with a virus that will end both their lives. God is in the cries heard under the rubble of war. God is in the debris of wasted opportunity and lives, and God is with us if we are with them. . . . It's not a coincidence that in the Scriptures, poverty is mentioned more than 2,100 times. It's not an accident. That's a lot of airtime, 2,100 mentions.
—Bono, "VERBATIM"

Jesus's resurrection is the beginning of God's new project not to snatch people away from earth to heaven but to colonize earth with the life of heaven. That, after all, is what the Lord's Prayer is about.

—N. T. Wright, *Surprised by Hope*

In 1986, I was working during the summer at the old Gesu parish in North Philadelphia, right next to the Jesuit high school I had attended. I was sitting on the stoop of the Jesuit house on North 18th St. talking with a young man from the neighborhood. We were talking about many things, and somewhere in the conversation he asked me why I was a Jesuit and why I wanted to be a priest. I told him Jesus had changed my life. "Do you know Jesus," I asked? He paused and thought, and then replied, "To tell you the truth, I never met the Dude."

Too many people today have not met "the Dude." Men know reams of statistics about their favorite sports teams; women can talk about the minutiae of wedding planning; people know how to work computers and figure out their taxes. We know way too much about flash-in-the-pan celebrities (e.g., Charlie Sheen, Lindsay Lohan, Snooki and the Situation, Miley Cyrus) while knowing little about the corporations that control our lives. And so many know next to nothing about the one many of us believe is the savior of the world and gateway to eternal life.

Even with popular culture's *GodSpell* and *Jesus Christ Superstar*, millions in what were once Christian lands know very little about the one who, arguably, is the most significant person in human history. Even if you are not a believing Christian, you should know something about Jesus. Maybe the average guy in the United States knows as little about Muhammad as the average young man in Saudi Arabia knows about Jesus, but I bet the average guy in a Muslim land knows a lot more about the prophet than the average American Joe knows about the one we believe to be the Son of God, our Lord.

Jesus is fascinating on so many levels. Born to unknown simple folk in what would be the Appalachian region of Israel, raised in a small, nondescript village ("Can anything good come from Nazareth?" [John 1:46]), Jesus bursts onto the scene somewhere around thirty years of age. He gathers a like-minded band of disciples who are intent on preaching the inbreaking of the reign of God. Splitting the political difference between those in Israel who would kowtow to Roman oppressors and cooperate with them, and those who wanted to indulge in bloody and ultimately futile rebellion against Caesar's minions, Jesus describes a way of life that transcends and subverts the political and religious cultures of his times. His beatitudes and parables call for a radically new form of life, one rooted in relationships of justice, relationships that overturn the ways people understand God, family, and their very selves. Jesus has and shares an experience of God who is Father, Abba ("Daddy"), a God who comes close and empowers us to heal one another and our societal sins and social ills.

All too soon Jesus is crushed in the complex currents of his times. Jesus and his band of rough, uneducated fishermen, tax collectors, and, scandalously, women (Luke 8:1), head for the big city, Jerusalem. Imagine a bunch of shrimpers from Louisiana's Gulf Coast in Los Angeles or the Duck Dynasty guys in Manhattan. Rather than flee trouble and hide back in Galilee, Jesus "sets his face" and marches to Jerusalem where he realizes the confrontation with the religious authorities is inevitable (see Luke 9:51). Overturning the money lenders' tables in the temple (much like pulling the plug on Wall Street's computers) calls down the wrath of the powerful. Soon he is imprisoned and charged with sedition. He is categorized as a threat to Caesar, forcing Pilate's hand, and getting the Galilean preacher condemned to be crucified. He dies an ignominious and horribly painful death, hung on the cross between two other *lēstai*, a Koine Greek word meaning not "thieves" but "bandits," "insurrectionists," those opposed to Roman rule. The *New American Bible* boldly states that Jesus was crucified with two "revolutionaries" (Matt 28:38). Imagine how differently the promise "You will be with me this day in paradise" sounds when it's addressed to the "good revolutionary" rather than the "good thief." Crucifixion was the Roman world's punishment for those who threatened revolt. The sign above Jesus named his crime. He was INRI (*Iesus Nazarenus Rex Iudaeorum*), "Jesus the Nazarene, King of the Jews."

In the 2013 History Channel presentation *The Bible*, there is a scene where the somewhat Malibu-surfer-looking Jesus looks at Peter after the miraculous catch of fish (see Luke 5) and says to him, "Come on. We're going to change the world."

That's exactly what happened. Jesus' followers began to change the world. Whatever the resurrection was and is, there is no doubt that Peter and Mary Magdalene, and soon St. Paul, went about preaching "Jesus is risen." In Christ, in the Messiah, the anointed one, we have access to forgiveness of our sins and radical transformation through the power of the Holy Spirit. In the early decades of the Jesus movement, the majority of believers were slaves and outcasts of society, the ones Jesus himself enjoyed hanging out with, sharing their lives and their food at table. The Roman Empire tried to destroy the fledgling religion, sending Christians to the lions. But the blood of martyrs waters the tree of faith. In a few hundred years, the emperor Constantine would make Christianity the religion of the realm, which may have been a mixed blessing.

No matter how you understand and evaluate the convoluted and complex history of Christianity, there is no doubt it all goes back to Jesus, to who he was, and what he did. Most importantly for us today, it goes back to what he said. The only way we know his words is through the writings of the New Testament. There was no YouTube in Jesus' day. The Sermon on the Mount was not televised and caught on tape. Jesus did not write a book, nor did he text.

A young Jesuit (when did I cease being one?) described something I had forgotten I'd said. He came to me as a college student who was thinking about becoming a Jesuit. In a story on Jesuit vocations for one of our magazines, he remembers my saying to him, "Look, Vinny. If you want to serve Jesus in the Jesuits, you've got to get to know Jesus. Read the Gospels." Vinny went and read the Gospels and his life was transformed. Something happened to him as Jesus came alive through the miracle of scripture. Vinny felt on fire to serve others as

Jesus would want us to do. Vinny will be ordained a Jesuit priest in a few years.

That's how it happens. Somebody tells somebody, "Get to know Jesus." They get to know Jesus and choices change, fires smoldering in hearts burst into flames of love and peace and justice. Old ways and false desires are burned away. Fire makes ashes; it also makes steel. As we get to know Jesus, the fire of the Holy Spirit burns within us and we see Jesus in the breaking of the bread, the same way it happened to the disciples on the road to Emmaus (Luke 24:13-35). We are formed into the community called church.

Read the Bible. Get to know Jesus. If you want to know who Jesus was, you have to know Moses and David and the great Jewish prophets. Pray the psalms, which were the prayer songs Jesus prayed. Listen to St. Paul and the others who first figured out what life in Christ means.

No one gets to know Jesus alone. We meet and deepen our relationship with Jesus in communion with others who also believe and who also search and study, trying to figure out how to live Jesus' message today. The Eucharist is the center and summit of Catholic life, for it is here that we gather and sacramentally experience the fire of the living God come down on the altar in consecrated bread and wine, which become Jesus' body and blood for us and the whole world. The receiving of Jesus in the Eucharist is food for our journey and connection with our Lord

One side note: Some complain about Catholics not sharing communion with others. If the consecrated host is seen as the cookie at the end of the meal, sure it's pretty insulting to say to someone invited to dinner, "You can't have that." To explain this practice, I tell college students, the reception of communion by Catholics is more like a fraternity or sorority pin, than dessert. Reception of communion at Mass (Catholics do not "take" communion; we "receive" communion) is a sign that one is trying to live our Catholic way of life. In the same way that you can go to the frat house and enjoy the party, you can share in our eucharistic celebration (as radically different as those social contexts actually are). But in the same way that you don't wear the frat pin unless you join the fraternity, we ask that those who are not Catholic refrain from reception of communion. I often invite those not receiving to come forward and receive a blessing.

There is much that unites Christians of various denominations. Most mainstream Christian churches agree on much that needs to be done to build a world of justice and peace and love. Catholic social teaching is a powerful analytic tool, helping us know how to implement the teaching of Jesus in the social and cultural contexts, and the political economies of our days.

How are we to forgive as the generous Father forgives the knucklehead younger son? How do we avoid becoming stupid, selfish, and hard of heart like the elder brother? (Luke 15:11-32). How do we embody and live the truths of the Beatitudes, knowing as Jesus did that the poor, the hungry, those who weep, those persecuted and despised are blessed, while the rich, the full, those happy and admired should be worried? (Luke 6:20-26). How do we live the truth that peacemakers, not warmongers, are like Jesus; that those who love rather than retaliate against enemies are Jesus' friends? How in our world so characterized by the gap between rich and poor do we live the teaching that those who serve the hungry and thirsty, the naked and imprisoned, those who notice the beggar at the door, are more like Jesus than those who ignore and despise the poor and dispossessed? (see Matt 25:31-46 or Luke 16:19-31).

What does it mean to be on fire with love for the poor and marginalized the way Jesus was? Eucharistic Prayer for Various Needs IV, "Jesus Who Went About Doing Good," prays: "He always showed compassion for children and for the poor, for the sick and for sinners, and he became a neighbor to the oppressed and the afflicted." Later in the prayer we hear, "Open our eyes to the needs of our brothers and sisters; inspire in us words and actions to comfort those who labor and are burdened. Make us serve them truly, after the example of Christ and at his command. And may your Church stand as a living witness to truth and freedom, to peace and justice, that all people may be raised up to a new hope."

Certainly Jesus wants us, like St. Francis, to rebuild our broken and battered church. If you had told me in 2001 what was going to descend on us, as horrific crimes against children perpetrated by priests came to light in the media (and don't blame the media—there's no sense in shooting the messenger), I would have figured it was time to get my truck driver's license and look for work. It is amazing, mind boggling, and humbling to me that so many have stuck with us through the horror and humiliations of the revelations since 2002. But it's all about Jesus. He calls sinners. We are a church of sorrowful sinners, not a showcase for saints. There are many young people who, despite the fact that some 4 percent of priests were involved in such atrocities, still find in the church the reality of the Body of Christ, serving in the world today. Many recognize that 96 percent of priests and 99.9 percent of sisters had nothing to do with the criminal, sinful, and, frankly, sickening sexual abuse of children. No one ever said being a disciple of Christ would be easy. Both those abused and those who abused are still our brothers and sisters in Christ.

And God save us from misguided Christians, those who think trying to refute evolution serves God, or killing abortion doctors is the way to make people see the evil of destroying unborn children. Jesus wants to change the world by transforming us into people who are lovers, intelligent and effective lovers. Jesus needs lovers who will allow themselves to be changed and set on fire with the passion of God to form a world of peace and prosperity, justice and joy, faith and freedom, hope and healing, love and life. Jesus wanted to change the world in his time, and he wants us to change our world today.

Jesus lived in a world where the Roman Empire dominated and controlled the people of Israel. The Herodians were the puppet rulers for the Roman overlords. King Herod, a ruthless despot who would kill a city's baby boys at the hint of a threat to his power, was succeeded by his sons. Herod Antipas was given rule over Galilee, a region known for producing rebels against the Romans and agents of Herod who maintained a system of corruption and extortion of the people. When Jesus was three or four years old, King Herod died. Rebellion erupted in many parts of Israel. A center of rebel activity was Sepphoris, a town of some 8,000 located five kilometers from Nazareth. Quintilus Varus, the governor of Syria, unleashed hell, like

Russell Crowe in *Gladiator*. With a force of twenty thousand, Varus regained control of Jerusalem, in the process crucifying some two thousand revolutionaries. Galilee was the main focus of the rebellion, so the Romans sacked Sepphoris and burned the city to the ground. As a child, Jesus would have heard the stories of these Roman atrocities. When Jesus spoke of "those who lord it over them," these are the images of illegitimate authority he would have in mind (see Pagola 2012, 36-37). And when he said his followers must take up their cross and follow him, he was being deadly serious.

Jesus preached the inbreaking of the reign of God, which meant huge changes for everyone and everything. Steeped in the meanings and promises of the Hebrew Scriptures, Jesus lived the life of a traveling preacher, dependent on the daily hospitality of those who invited him to their table and sheltered him from the elements. His down-to-earth preaching style and the authenticity of his personal presence attracted people in large crowds. Here was a teaching for which they hungered and thirsted without even knowing their spiritual malnourishment (John 4:1-42). In a world where family was everything, and often exclusive and selfish (it's all about "my" or "our" family/clan; forget others), his celibate lifestyle evidenced a new freedom and witnessed to the complete dedication of his life to the work of proclaiming the kingdom (Lohfink 2012, 226-29; Pagola 2012, 70-73). His powerful parables touched minds and hearts and set people on fire with the hopes hidden deep in the communal imagination of the people of Israel. Jesus lived most of his life in Galilee, an area more like rural West Virginia than Washington, D.C. As the news of his miracles and healings spread, the rulers of his society began to notice and react. John the Baptist was assassinated for criticizing the marriage of Herod. John's critique was more about the political alliance Herod made through the marriage than a condemnation of sexual impropriety. John's preaching threatened political powers, and those powers too often solve what they perceive to be problems by violently repressing those who disagree with the oppressive powers' political policies, choices, and actions.

There's been an idea floating around the past few decades that

Jesus' miracles can be explained in ways more acceptable to those of us born in post-Enlightenment and scientific cultural worlds. The multiplication of the loaves, the only miracle attested to by all four Gospels, was really people just sharing the food they had carried with them. People weren't really healed of demonic possession. They were what we would call epileptics or schizophrenics. More recent biblical scholarship is swinging the pendulum back the other way. Jesus really did enact extraordinary signs, miracles that radically changed peoples' lives, giving them health and freedom (see Lohfink 2012; Meier, 1994).

"For Jesus, the kingdom of God meant a revolution in the way people behaved toward each other" (Horsley and Silberman 1997, 54). The Roman oppressors, the temple authorities, and the zealots all were challenged by Jesus and threatened by peoples' adherence to his teachings. Jesus was a prophet, one in the line of Isaiah, Jeremiah, and Micah. Central passages from Daniel ("Son of Man" or "the Human One") and Isaiah ("Suffering Servant") informed Jesus' consciousness and led him to see himself as a new and different kind of anointed one, or Messiah. He realized that armed insurrection against the Roman oppressors was futile. Israel's fighters would be crushed like bugs on a car windshield by the Roman Empire's military machine. The temple was the center of Jesus' people's political and religious (often synonymous in Jesus' time and world) power and authority. The temple was much more like a small college campus than the local synagogue one sees in a U.S. city. The temple authorities were as interested in keeping things the way they were as their Roman overseers.

The social changes going on in Jesus' lifetime cried out to God. Poor people were being taxed off their land. Herod Antipas demanded two hundred talents a year in taxes. A talent was an enormous sum of money, worth six thousand days' wages (Pilch 1995, 137). The rich were getting richer and the poor poorer. "So the rich get rich and the poor they lose, so the Bible says, but it still is news . . ." goes the old song. "Jesus suggested that God was establishing His Kingdom by creating an alternative society. What kind of society was it? . . . Under the pressure of Herodian taxation and land dispossession, they had slipped away from a traditional village spirit of mutual cooperation. . . . Roman legal standards, not the Torah, began to take precedence" (Horsley and Silberman 1997, 54-55). Jesus saw village people who used to live in a spirit of cooperation set against one another by the social and economic forces bearing down upon them. Instead of banding together to help one another, people were becoming selfish, looking out for number one, and the hell with everyone else. Jesus' preaching, teachings, and miracles were not simply abstract spiritual truths. What he did was much more like "a program of community action and practical resistance to a system that efficiently transformed close-knit villages into badly fragmented communities of alienated, frightened individuals" (Horsley and Silberman 1997, 55).

Jesus spent his public life under death threats (see Mark 3:6). In the same way that Martin Luther King knew there were those who wanted to kill him for his championing of civil rights for African Americans in the United States, so too Jesus realized the dangers he and his disciples faced daily by preaching a gospel of peace and love and justice in worlds ruled by Rome's interests and the temple priesthood. Jesus' ideas and ways of being inevitably brought him into conflict with the powerful social institutions of his day. The Herodians wanted to kill him from the start. In John's Gospel, Jesus throws over the money changers' tables at the start of his public ministry (John 2:13-22). The powers of darkness decide early on to kill him.

Crucifixion was Rome's version of preventive punishment. The cross was the first-century electric chair. Comedian Lenny Bruce once reportedly said, "If Jesus had been killed twenty years ago, Catholic school children would be wearing little electric chairs around their necks instead of crosses." But the threat of crucifixion was not to keep only murderers and such in line; crucifixion was a message that this is what happens to you if you oppose Roman rule. Crucifixion was for those Rome ruled, for slaves and non-Romans. Normally, Roman citizens could not be crucified. As a little boy, Jesus would have heard of the hundreds crucified in Galilee (Lohfink 2012; Pagola 2012). "Crucifixion was as much communal punishment and state sponsored terrorism as it was judicial vengeance against a particular crime. The crosses planted outside the cities warned potential rebels, runaway slaves, and rebellious prophets of what could happen to *them*" (Horsley and Silberman 1997, 86).

Jesus suffered a horrific death. We love and follow a crucified God. We need to reflect often on the implications of that fact of our faith.

> There should be no question or mystery about the brutality of the Roman crucifixion. . . . All over the Mediterranean world, Roman emperors, governors, prefects and procurators had the power, and even the responsibility, to inflict unspeakable pain and physical suffering on any person whom their officers grabbed from the fields or the streets and identified—rightly or wrongly—as a threat to private property, public order or state security. The horrible, prolonged process of crucifixion was described in detail. . . . The condemned person would be stripped naked and humiliated in public and scourged soundly by soldiers with metal-tipped leather lashes. Then, forced to carry a heavy transverse beam, or *patibulum*, to the place of execution, the victim was brutally hung up on the vertical post. And he would remain there, guarded by soldiers, for as long as it took to die of his wounds or succumb to the asphyxiation caused by the sagging weight of his exhausted body—which was bound to the rough wooden cross with ropes or affixed there with jagged iron nails. (Horsley and Silberman 1997, 85)

As I said, we have to meditate long and hard on the fact that we follow a crucified God. That Jesus suffered a shameful and torturous death on the cross has much to say about the mystery of suffering. The crucifixion also has much to say about social sin and the consequences of societies and cultures being set up and organized in ways that benefit the few while the many go hungry, uneducated, and without health care or social security.

St. Paul's insights led to the awareness that the crucifixion of Jesus changed the meaning of the cross. Jesus could easily have avoided crucifixion. He could have hid out in Galilee. He prayed in Gethsemane that this cup pass him by. Yet he allowed himself to be taken, tortured, and killed. Jesus' being willing to undergo death on the cross was a declaration to Rome that those who accepted and entered the kingdom of God would no longer go along with the injustices of the Roman Empire. For St. Paul, "The cross became the symbol both of Roman violence and those who dared to resist its inevitability" (Horsley and Silberman 1997, 161). The cross also became the way Paul called to people caught up in ways of living that destroyed their hopes of personal and societal transformation. Participation in the mystery of Christ's cross promised new and better ways of being persons.

> The vices he [St. Paul] railed against—"immorality, impurity, licentiousness, idolatry, sorcery, enmity, strife, jealousy, anger, selfishness, dissension, party spirit, envy, drunkenness, carousing, and the like" (Gal 5:19-21)—were the kinds of behavior that were all too common among the powerless subjects of the empire. Unless his followers abandoned them, they would remain helpless to effect or be part of any world transforming change. In that sense, the image of Jesus offered a model of practical self-sacrifice in the cause of the economic and spiritual resurrection for communities that were being scourged, mocked and dismembered by imperial rule. (Horsley and Silberman 1997, 160-61)

Of course, the even more fascinating reality for long and hard meditation is the fact of the resurrection. Again, in response to those scholars who wonder if the resurrection was only the birth of faith among his disciples in ongoing presence of Jesus, more recent scholarship is shifting back to the argument that there really was an empty tomb, that something unique and transformative on the cosmic level occurred after the crucifixion (see Lohfink 2012; Meier 1994; Wright 1999; 2011). The Gospels provide us with stylized and theologically constructed accounts, not history in the sense we understand history in the twenty-first century. But the idea that all that occurred was in the minds and hearts of the disciples, with no "real" resurrection, is implausible. Heavyweight New Testament scholar Anglican bishop N. T. Wright counters scholars like Rudolf Bultmann and Edward Schillebeeckx, who wonder if the resurrection was just the disciples whipping up a communal fantasy of Jesus' continued presence. Wright writes, "I have to say that as a historian I find them [i.e., such theories] far harder to accept than the stories told by the evangelists themselves" (Wright 1999, 148). Wright argues that we have "to take seriously the witness of the whole early church, that Jesus of Nazareth was raised bodily to a new sort of life, three days after his execution" (1999, 148).

In his *Simply Jesus*, a stunning and original exposition of the meaning and message of Jesus, Wright argues forcefully that Jesus was all about reestablishing the people of Israel in contradistinction to, not simply against, the Roman Empire. For Wright, the cross is a new manner of exercising power (2011, 179). "Somehow Jesus' death was seen by Jesus himself . . . as the ultimate means by which God's kingdom was established" (p. 185). Easter is Jesus rising into the new world that Israel's God has always been intending to come into being.

The resurrection is really real! More real than real. Jesus is the new temple. In biblical thought "heaven and earth overlap and interlock, as the ancient Jews believed they did in the Temple" (Wright 2011, 192). The risen Jesus is the Christ present both here on earth and there in heaven. The new creation has begun. This new creation that has entered our world in and through Jesus is real, and its power is love (Wright 2011, 194). "Heaven permeates earth" and, since Jesus is now in heaven, he is thus every-where and every-when on earth" (Wright 2011, 196). Jesus is at work today, at work in the world in and through the church, the essential work of love and transformation that begins and is impelled by, and made real and present in and through, our acts of worship (see Wright 2011, 217, 227, 231).

The main thing to realize is that what happens to Jesus happens to us. St. Augustine said, "God became Man so that Man might become God." Every year we remember liturgically the great events of Jesus' life. A rabbi once said you could sum up all of scripture with one word: Remember!

Every Lent and Easter we re-member Jesus, who he was and is. We relive and re-present the events of the Last Supper and the crucifixion. We wait in the silence of Holy Saturday. And on Easter we rejoice. He is risen. He is truly risen! Our faith calls us to a promised future of a heavenly realm (see Romans 8 and Revelation 21) where every tear will be wiped away (Isa 25:8 and Rev 21:4), and God will be "all in all" (1 Cor 15:28).

Today's militant atheists say we are fools. Faith is ridiculous. Jesus died on the cross and that was it. Case closed. Death swallows us up in a meaningless, black void and we simply cease to exist. There's no difference between Mother Teresa and Hitler.

The truth is, Jesus is risen. Jesus lives. Jesus saves us. From all sin. From all suffering. From all injustice. Wars and weapons, horrors and hate, torture and terror fill the news. Teens, military personal, and now middle-aged people commit suicide at alarming rates. Human trafficking ensnares twenty-seven million, mostly young girls, in twenty-first-century forms of abject slavery. The never-ending revelations of priest sex abuse and the charges of bishops' covering up the sins/crimes goes on and on. Beyond comprehension, senseless shootings in places like Newtown, Connecticut, happen with numbing regularity. Wars go on and on with no end in sight in Afghanistan, Iraq, and other troubled areas. All the bad news. . . .

And then there are the personal tragedies and sadness of our days. A parent dies of cancer. Corporate malfeasance eliminates your job. A baseball player realizes he'll never make the majors. And, on a much more mundane level, it's another year when I didn't lose twenty-five pounds during Lent!

Into all the bad news and failures of the world comes Jesus. Jesus saves! Jesus is risen! He is truly risen! Alleluia! We share in his resurrection. This is what we celebrate on Easter. This is what we believe.

On Easter Sunday a few years ago, the congregation was responding loudly and enthusiastically, "We do," to the renewal of our baptismal vows. As the last "We do" resounded through the church, a small, three-year-old girl, held in her father's arms, let out with a perfectly timed, "I don't." All present cracked up laughing. It was funny. But it raises the question, what do we believe about the resurrection? What does Jesus' resurrection mean for us?

Resurrection is not resuscitation or reanimation of a corpse. Resurrection is transformation. Resurrection is the promise of what will happen to those who die in Christ. Resurrection means "a complete transformation of the human being in his or her psychosomatic totality. . . . Resurrection was thought of not as an event for the individual at death but as a corporate event. God would raise all the elect at the end of history" (*Harper's Bible Dictionary*).

The Son of God became what we are so we might become what God is (see CCC §460). That's not some Jesuit spin on theology. That's St. Athanasius in the fourth century. Jesus' resurrection gives us the grace, that is, the power we need to be able to live with God forever.

Faith in the resurrection means that we believe in life beyond this life, and that eternal life begins not when we die but the moment we are baptized. We believe that the God who gives us existence and preserves us alive all our days will continue to give us the gift of life for all eternity. We know God has given us life now. Why would we assume that God would stop giving us life when our bodies die? It seems to me that it makes more sense to hope for life beyond death. After all, I'm alive now, and that's quite a miracle.

Science can tell us many things. But scientific truth has limits. Science can answer "how?" and "what?" but not "why?" and "what for?" There's scientific truth and there is also the truth of love and eternal life. Neither of those can be scientifically studied. Much of what really matters in life is not replicable. Dr. Eben Alexander, a neurosurgeon, was really not much of a believer before he suffered meningitis and went into a coma. He wrote *Proof of Heaven*, sharing his experiences of life beyond this life (www.lifebeyonddeath.net). Dr. Raymond Moody has been studying the reality of "Life after Life" for more than fifty years (http://www.lifeafterlife.com). But even testimony of those who have survived near-death experiences only gives us a hint. They can make the hope of resurrection and eternal life a bit more plausible. But only faith can tell what awaits us beyond the grave.

Life eternal is not like a change of horses where we ride off into a far distant sunset on another stallion. Karl Rahner, the great Jesuit theologian, taught that the resurrection means that we become all we could ever have been. All the limits of this life are lifted and we are all we could ever hope and desire to be (Rahner 1967, 156).

According to Jesuit David Stanley, the resurrection means that the kingdom of God has arrived on this earth. New Testament authors intimate that heaven means we join Jesus in his reign over the "course of world history. Heaven . . . is not a kind of perennial 'Old Folks Home.' It is not simply a place of retirement and celestial repose for senior citizens of the kingdom of God. . . . heaven consists in the active participation in the glorified Christ's direction of history" (Stanley 1967, 282-84).

We remember, when we celebrate Easter, that transformation in Jesus is what our lives are all about. We are all heading for eternal life.

All of us have lost loved ones. Where are they? How are they? Rahner writes, "The great mistake of many people . . . is to imagine that those whom death has taken, leave us. They do not leave us. They remain! Where are they? In the darkness? Oh, no. It is we who are in darkness. We do not see them, but they see us. Their eyes radiant with glory, are fixed upon our eyes. . . . Though invisible to us, our dead are not absent. . . . They are living near us transfigured into light and power and love" (quoted in Livingston 2006).

How can we believe this good news, this wonderful revelation of our God of love? Pray. Prayer reveals reality to us. Thomas Merton wrote, "Prayer is a real source of personal freedom in the midst of a world in which men are dominated by massive organizations and rigid institutions which seek only to exploit them for money and power. Far from being a source of alienation, true religion in spirit is a liberating force that helps man to find himself in God" (in Bochen 2000, 37).

Prayer makes us remember Jesus and allows the fire of the Holy Spirit to glow within us. There's a story about an eighty-three-year-old widower. He met an eighty-one-year-old woman who also had lost her spouse. They hit it off, began to spend a lot of time with each other, and, after some months, he decided to ask her to marry him. He takes her out to a nice restaurant and over coffee and dessert, pops the question. With tears of joy in her eyes, she says, "Yes." The next day he wakes up and can't remember her answer. He calls her and asks if she said yes. She's so relieved and tells him, "I'm so glad you called. I know I said I'd marry someone last night, but I couldn't remember to whom I'd been speaking."

The church helps us re-member Jesus, who he was and who he is. The church keeps alive, tangible, and real the presence of Christ. We are his body in the world today. He works through us. The Holy Spirit of love that the Father and Son sends into our hearts (Rom 5:5) sets us on fire.

How do we do in our time what Jesus did in his? Kurt Vonnegut, the famous zany and imaginative novelist, once noted that many fervent Christians want the Ten Commandments posted in courtrooms. "And of course, that's Moses, not Jesus. I haven't heard one of them demand that the Sermon on the Mount, the Beatitudes, be posted anywhere. 'Blessed are the merciful' in a courtroom? 'Blessed are the peacemakers' in the Pentagon? Give me a break!" (Vonnegut, *A Man without a Country*). To do what Jesus did, we join the people who are doing what he is doing. We give ourselves to and immerse ourselves in his body, the Body of Christ, the church as it is, with all its warts and wobbles. We risk aligning ourselves in community and allowing God to do through us what God desires done in our world.

CHAPTER 4

Christ Is Community

A word from Charles Schulz's Peanuts. Charlie Brown has his head back and mouth wide open. Linus smiles and says, "Happiness is singing in the choir." In another cartoon Linus is yelling in one panel, "I love mankind. It's people I can't stand."

Mechanically, we have gained in the last generation, but spiritually, we have, I think, unwittingly, lost. In other times, women had in their lives more forces which centered them whether or not they realized it. . . . The church too, has always been a great centering force for women. Through what ages women have had that quiet hour, free of interruption, to draw themselves together. No wonder woman has been the mainstay of the church. . . . The church is still a great centering force for men and women, more needed now than ever before . . . but are those who attend as ready to give themselves or to receive its message as they used to be? Our daily life does not prepare us for contemplation. How can a single weekly hour of church, helpful as it may be, counteract the many daily hours of distraction that surround it? . . . For the need for renewal is still there. The desire to be accepted as whole, the desire to be seen as an individual, and not as a collection of functions, the desire to give oneself completely and purposefully pursues us always.

—Lindbergh, *Gift from the Sea*, 52-55

The task of the Christian is to cooperate with God in bringing the world back to God.

—Baldovin, *Bread of Life*, xiii-xiv

Anne Morrow Lindbergh recognized almost sixty years ago the distracted, disintegrating, destabilized lives we were creating with our gadgets and time-saving mechanical devices. What would she say of our contemporary world of cell phones with 24/7 texting and ephemeral, constant communication? She would note that we are in electronic contact but we more and more lack the ability to really connect with one another or even slow down and reflect in order to pay attention to what is going on inside us. College students today are much more impressed by the fact that Jesuits make two thirty-day silent retreats and annual eight-day retreats in silence than they are by the religious vows we profess. We all need the connectedness and community that a church tradition offers, when lived and practiced long term and lovingly. Christ is community and community is crucial. Community takes effort but can make us happy and holy, saintly and sane.

A guy goes to the supermarket and notices a very attractive young woman waving at him. She says, "Hello." He's rather taken aback because he can't place from where he knows her. So he asks, "Do you know me?" She replies, "You're the father of one of my kids." Now his mind travels back to the only two times he has ever been unfaithful to his wife. So he gets all red in the face, stammers and asks, "Are you the gal from accounting who I met in the cloak room when I got drunk at the company Christmas party in 2007?" She replies, "No." Are you the gal at the company picnic out at Lake Whoopee in 2009?" "No," she says. He stammers, "Well look . . ." She looks into his eyes and says calmly, "I'm your son's second-grade teacher."

This wouldn't happen in a world where we naturally formed better communities. Unlike most of human history, we live in societies where we cannot recognize the vast majorities of people we see each day. From tribes and small villages, we have come to live in cities populated by millions of people we never know and rarely, if ever, meet.

The church in our times is more necessary than ever, for modern mass societies of anonymous, disconnected individuals need institutions that create community across demographic, ethnic, cultural, and political divides. I learned much of the power and beauty of community at the first parish to which I was sent.

On warm, windy April evenings, or blustery cold March nights, we would celebrate Holy Saturday at Holy Name Parish, 5th and Vine Streets in Camden, New Jersey. The streets surrounding the church are some of the most distressed in the United States. Depending on the year, Camden has often been named the poorest city in the country, and/or the most dangerous. I was welcomed into this wonderful parish family right after I was ordained in 1988. For the next fifteen years, every year the community would join together liturgically to celebrate the Triduum. Holy Thursday was often combined with an actual meal. On Good Friday, the people carried a huge cross through the streets as the priest led the crowds in the Stations of the Cross. Many of the scenes of the Way of the Cross were correlated with happenings in North Camden during the past year. We would pray on well-known drug corners, at sites where people were murdered, and at vacant lots filled with the remains of houses that had burned down months or years before. Throughout the city, Catholic communities carried the cross to places that symbolized the way the city was mistreated by the larger society: for example, the county sewage plant that was foisted on the city or the Canadian cement company that set up their dust-spewing business in South Camden, a community where kids' asthma rates are much higher than those in places like the nearby affluent suburban communities of Cherry Hill or Voorhees.

The cross is all too well known in Camden, and the violence and poverty of the city are too often highlighted by the mass media practicing "Oh My God!" journalism. The reporters come in and export an image of Camden that shocks and elicits some pity, but very rarely leads to any positive transformation. Outsiders very rarely are aware of the exuberant joy of little kids playing Tee Ball on May evenings (the funniest thing in three states), or people like Cristobal and Norberta who raised ten children in North Camden and saw nine of them graduate from college and the other one join the Camden police force.

The community at Holy Name created a space where people felt loved and accepted and cherished by God, and the guy or gal in the pew next to them. It is this community that is the visible, tangible continuance of the fire of Holy Saturday—even on the Holy Saturday that we lit the fire inside because of rain. It set off the fire alarm and the fire engines screamed up to the church as the *Exsultet* was being sung! On most Holy Saturdays, over a dozen little kids were ready to be baptized, the girls in flowing white dresses and the little guys in white tuxes or snazzy black and grey slacks and shirt outfits bought new at Kmart or Target.

What a good parish does is give people not just a sense, not just a taste, but an actual, ongoing, tangible experience of community. Holy Name in Camden was, for me and for so many, a source of hope and courage in a neighborhood stricken by the social ills that come in the wake of living in a severely economically distressed inner city. Despite the drug dealing and deaths, the pain and the poverty, people at Holy Name banded together to form a community. We had the Hijas de Maria club for girls and young women, Little League, Quinceañera celebrations, and parish dances with everyone from eight months to eighty in attendance. We had beautiful baptisms, lovely weddings, and moving funerals. The Sunday eucharistic celebration was the central point of the week. Sometimes the Mass would take ninety minutes, but no one was in any hurry.

No one comes to know Jesus without a community. Even if one simply picks up the New Testament and begins reading, the fact that there is a collection of first-century writings attesting to who and what Jesus is, and what he said, is evidence that our relationship with Jesus is based on the communities that produced those Gospels and epistles.

Jesus came that we might "have life and have it to the full" (John 10:10). In order to have such life, we need community. Our overly individualistic culture teaches us the lie that each of us can take care of ourselves. Certainly, at the start and usually in the last years of life, the radical nature of our dependence on one another is self-evident. And some simple reflection exposes the lie that I can take care of myself. We can be so blind to the millions of people on whom we depend every day. Without those who grow and provide our food we would starve. Without all who make civil society function, from the mayor and fire companies and police departments, to the hospitals and schools and sanitation engineers, to the municipal water departments, our lives would soon be living hells. Ever live through a strike by garbage collectors in a major U.S. city? In summer time? I did once in Philadelphia. It wasn't pretty, and the smell . . . Enough said. How long could you exist without clean and trustworthy water supplies? We need one another. We cannot survive without one another. To suggest otherwise is ludicrous.

Community takes work, lots of work. Community necessitates a great deal of commitment, self-sacrifice, and forgiveness. St. John Berchmans, a seventeenth-century Jesuit saint, is reputed to have said, "I engage in no great penances. Community life is enough." Catholicism is a community-based and a community-oriented way of living. You can't celebrate Eucharist alone.

Eucharist is inherently communally formed and fashioned. We become what we receive, that is, the body of Christ. The Catholic faithful participate in these processes of receiving God's gifts and sharing those gifts with one another by celebrating the communal meal Jesus celebrated as he prepared to suffer on the cross. It is when we come together to enact the Eucharist that we are transformed and go forth to transform our world.

> The transformation in question is most of all our transformation. . . . we speak of the transformation of the gifts of bread and wine into the body and blood of Christ so that ultimately we are transformed into the Body and Blood of Christ for the world. That is why the great St. Augustine was able to tell his hearers in Hippo: "There is your mystery on the table. Be what you receive." In other words, we need to think of communion *both* as our receiving the living Lord *and* as the Body of Christ incorporating us. We receive Christ into our bodies and Christ

receives us into his body—the Church, which is his sacrament in the world. (Baldovin 2003, 157-58)

Receiving communion in a Catholic church is a sign of commitment to and belief in the Catholic way of life. College students often wonder why the church doesn't invite everyone to receive. I tell them it's a question of the cultural meaning of what is being signified by reception of communion. If you are invited to someone's home for dinner and they say, "Oh, you're welcome to join us at the table, but you can't have dessert," that's pretty insulting. If communion is seen as the cookie at the end of the meal, refusal to share seems the antithesis of charity and community. But communion is much more like a fraternity or sorority pin. You can go to the frat party (not recommended by those of us who teach college students, and I know what I'm talking about—I was in Delta Upsilon at Lafayette College in the mid-1970s). But you don't wear the pin unless you join the frat and pledge to be a member of the house.

Receiving communion is not an individualistic action. Receiving, not taking, communion is a communal sign and experience. Thomas Merton decades ago pushed against a too-individualistic sense of communion.

It is also important that in order to purify our hearts and enter more perfectly into the joy of Communion with the Risen Christ, we should strive to free ourselves from the narrow limitations of an individualistic piety which treats Communion as a refuge from the troubles and sorrows of communal living and ends by cutting us off spiritually from the Mystical Christ. There is an unconscious and unrecognized infantilism which moves some pious souls to treat Communion uniquely as a source of personal consolation—their meeting with the Eucharistic Christ is regarded solely as an occasion to plunge into the darkness and sweetness of their own subjectivity, and rest in the forgetfulness of all else. . . . But to make Communion a refuge from reality, from social responsibility, from the pain of being a mature person, is in fact to withdraw from Christ into the darkness and inertia of our own subjectivity. Communion is not a flight from life, not an evasion of reality, but the full acceptance of our membership in Christ and the total commitment of ourselves to the lives and aims of the Mystical Body of Christ. (Merton 1956, 86-87)

Community consists in a set of social structures. I played football from the time I was seven on into college. It's a great game. I loved it. Nothing was more fun than running around smashing into one another. It was best played in rain and mud. I was a center on offense and an inside linebacker on defense. In all those years, I scored one touchdown. I intercepted a pass during a scrimmage against Archbishop Ryan and ran it into the end zone for a score. Even though I was a good player, it was pretty much impossible for someone in my position to score touchdowns. The game was structured to allow the backs and receivers to score the TDs and get the glory. In a weird way, team sports are very communal and communistic social systems. Karl Marx said that a good and just society would be one where everyone gives according to their abilities and takes according to their needs. Although the linemen and defensive players don't get as much glory, or, in the pros, money, as the quarterbacks, they still give 110% for the success of the team.

Virtually all of us are communists. I often say this to college students and they look at me with great skepticism. But I ask them, "Did you ever live in a society where everyone gives according to their abilities and takes according to their needs?" Their immediate response is, "No." I then gently suggest, "Don't you all come from families? Doesn't your family operate on the principle that everyone gives according to their abilities and takes according to their needs? Does your family charge the little kids for the food they eat? Are you going to get a bill for services rendered when you reach the age of eighteen?" One economist once admitted the inherent logic of my argument, but immediately observed, "It all depends on how large you want to make that family circle."

A church based on community made up of people on fire with the transformative love of Christ wants to make that circle as large as the entire human race, the whole family of all of us on earth. The great and charismatic apostle to the gang members of Los Angeles, Jesuit Greg Boyle, preaches we are all "kin." Having reintegrated thousands of gang members back into family, community, and businesses after their time in the gang life and/or stints in prison, Greg teaches, "We would have a lot more Justice if we saw one another as kin." He is so correct.

Our ever more globalized society is set up in ways that militate against the practice of community. Corporate capitalism doesn't make the other "kin"; corporate capitalism makes the "other" the competitor, if not the enemy. Wages are set on anything but a rational basis. I don't care how good a teacher you are; you will never become rich from your salary. You can be the best math teacher in the history of the world, but you will never make what a hedge fund manager or a professional athlete makes. Wages and rewards in the corporate capitalistic system are structured to erode if not destroy community. "If you keep your food in a fridge, your clothes in a closet, have a roof over your head and sleep in a bed you are wealthier than seventy-five percent of the world's population. If you have a bank account, you are among the wealthiest eight percent of the world" (Privett 2003, 12). So few have so much and so many have so little.

St. Augustine said, "The Father sent the Son into the world to defend the poor." In the United States, 46.2 million Americans were living below the poverty line in 2011. Fifteen percent of the population is poor (15.2% in 2010 but 11.3% in 2000). The U.S. government sets the poverty line for a family of four at $23,021. There are 16.1 million children (21.9% of children in America) living in poverty; 7.6 million children (9.7%) do not have health insurance. The number of people without health coverage is 46.8 million (U.S. census 2012).

In 1987, the bishops of the United States proclaimed, "The needs of the poor take priority over the desires of the rich; the rights of workers over the maximization of profits; the preservation of the environment over uncontrolled industrial expansion; the production to meet social needs over production for military purposes" (USCCB 1986, §94). Economic inequality is a central challenge for the United States today and should be getting far more attention in presidential campaigns. "We cannot separate what we believe from how we act in the marketplace and the broader community, for this is where we make our primary contribution to the pursuit of economic justice" (USCCB 1986, §25). We cannot break bread at the altar of the Lord, the eucharistic table, and ignore the fact that millions of our sisters and brothers are suffering hunger. Noble Prize–winning economist Paul Krugman argues in the *New York Times* that too many politicians in the U.S. Congress take "positive glee in inflicting further suffering on the already miserable" (Krugman 2013). The Farm Bill passed by Congress in the summer of 2013 lavished billions on large agribusiness corporations while eviscerating the Supplemental Nutrition Assistance Program, or SNAP. "So House Republicans voted to maintain farm subsidies—at a higher level than either the Senate or the White House proposed—while completely eliminating food stamps from the bill" (Krugman 2013). $134 a month is the average a person receives in food stamp assistance. Tennessee Representative Stephen Fincher quoted the Bible saying those who won't work shall not eat. Fincher himself has taken millions in farm subsidies (Krugman 2013).

> To fully appreciate what just went down, listen to the rhetoric conservatives often use to justify eliminating safety-net programs. It goes something like this: "You're personally free to help the poor. But the government has no right to take people's money"—frequently, at this point, they add the words "at the point of a gun"—"and force them to give it to the poor." It is, however, apparently perfectly O.K. to take people's money at the point of a gun and force them to give it to agribusinesses and the wealthy. (Krugman 2013)

The great Canadian poet and folk singer Leonard Cohen best describes our situation in his mesmerizing song "Everybody Knows." "Everybody knows that the dice are loaded / Everybody rolls with their fingers crossed / Everybody knows that the war is over / Everybody knows the good guys lost / Everybody knows the fight was fixed / The poor stay poor, the rich get rich / That's how it goes / Everybody knows." The hope for Cohen is found in the power of the people to change social structures and cultural conditions. To a heart-thumping beat, Cohen sings his haunting anthem "Democracy": "It's coming from the sorrow on the street / The holy places where the races meet / from the homicidal bitchin' / That goes down in every kitchen / To determine who will serve and who will eat / from the wells of disappointment / Where the women kneel to pray / For the grace of God in the desert here / And the desert far away / Democracy is coming to the U.S.A." Will we vote to change things?

Pope John Paul II saw the need for change on multiple levels: "A change of mentality is needed, no longer seeing the poor as a burden, or as intruders trying to profit from others, but as people seeking to share the goods of the world so that we can create a just and prosperous world for all" (John Paul II, *Centesimus Annus*, 1991, §28). The prophetic pontiff speaking in the United States said:

> In the final analysis however, we must realize that social injustice and unjust social structures exist only because individuals and groups of individuals deliberately maintain and tolerate them. It is these personal choices, operating through structures that breed and propagate situations of poverty, oppression and misery. For this reason, overcoming "social" sin and reforming the social order itself must begin with the conversion of our hearts. As the American Bishops have said, "The Gospel confers on each Christian the vocation to love God and neighbor in ways that bear fruit in the life of society. That vocation consists above all in a change of heart: a conversion expressed in praise of God and in concrete deeds of justice and service. (Pope John Paul II 1987)

A few snapshots: In the United States, the top 1 percent hold more wealth than the bottom 90 percent combined (Kristof 2011). Six heirs of Sam Walton, the founder of Walmart, have as much wealth as the bottom 100 million Americans. In 2010, the top 1 percent got 93 percent of gains in national income. In September 2012, America's Gini coefficient, the classic measure of economic inequality, reached record levels—the highest seen since the Great Depression (Kristof 2012).

CEO pay is a prime indicator of how inequality grows like a cancer in our corporate capitalist economy. In 2012 the average CEO pay at 350 of the largest companies in the United States was 279.1 times the average worker's wage. That was less than the 384.1 times more than a worker's wage in 2000 but up from the 22.4 to 1 ratio of 1972 (Svaldi 2013). Lawrence Mishel, president of the Economic Policy Institute, states, "The shocking increase in CEO compensation is not really a reflection of the market demand for talent—it's the result of the fact that CEOs have considerable control of their own pay and significant incentives to demand a greater and greater share of company profits" (in Svaldi 2013). The ongoing discussion of CEO pay masks even greater inequalities in the supposedly rational market economy. Hedge fund managers make billions: "the top five hedge-fund managers make more than all the CEOs in the Standard & Poor's 500 combined" (Svaldi 2013). A *New York Times* editorial reports CEO median compensation was $15.1 million, up 16 percent since 2011. The editors note that the Economic Policy Institute found that "the ratio of C.E.O. pay to employee pay was 273 to 1 in 2012, or 202 to 1, depending on how stock options were accounted for. Either way, that is far higher than it has been for most of the past 50 years (*New York Times*, editorial, July 14, 2013).

Harvard professor Michael Sandel points out, "In 2004-2006, the average CEO in the U.S. made $13.3 million annually. Schoolteachers average $43,000 a year; David Letterman takes $31 million. Chief Justice John Roberts gets $217,000; Judge Judy walks away with $25 million" (Sandel 2009, 162).

Globally, 80 percent of the people on the planet live on less than ten dollars a day. Across our planet, twenty-one thousand children die each day from preventable causes. Almost 30 percent of little kids in developing countries are underweight. We could have taken less than 1 percent of what the world spends on weapons and placed every child in school by the year 2000, but we didn't do so. Seventy-two million kids around the world are not in school; more than half of them are girls (http://www.globalissues.org/article/26/poverty-facts-and-stats). Nicholas Kristof and Sheryl WuDunn note that societies that educate and empower girls disempower terrorists (2009, xxi).

The Millennium Project reports that one billion people strive to survive on less than one dollar a day and another 2.7 billion live on less than two dollars a day. This poverty includes the hardship of having to walk a mile to haul water or firewood. Such poverty means that children, eleven million a year, are dying from diseases like malaria, diarrhea, and pneumonia—ailments eradicated years ago in the developed world. Annually, malnutrition kills six million little kids before they reach the age of five. Every half minute an African child dies of malaria. That's more than a million a year. Some 800 million people suffer hunger daily; 300 million of them are children who try to go to sleep as their stomachs cry for food. Forty percent of people on this planet don't have the simple pleasure of having a latrine. "A woman living in sub-Saharan Africa has a 1 in 16 chance of dying in pregnancy or childbirth. This compares with a 1 in 3,700 risk for a woman in North America" (http://www.unmillenniumproject.org/documents/3-MP-PovertyFacts-E.pdf).

The Catholic vision is that we are all brothers and sisters. As Jesuit father Greg Boyle preaches, "We are all kin." As Catholics, we were singing "We are Family" long before Sister Sledge made the phrase a hit. By the power of the Holy Spirit, Jesus lives within us, making us his Body, the Body of Christ in the World today. Through us, Jesus the Christ continues his presence and action in the world, action inspired and sustained by the Holy Spirit to the glory of God the Father. Together, we are called to do something beautiful for God, as journalist Malcom Muggeridge said of Mother Teresa.

There's the story of a man walking by a construction site. He sees a man looking at blueprints and asks what he's doing. "I'm working,"

From *Catechism of the Catholic Church*

"Social Justice can be obtained only in respecting the transcendent dignity of man. The person represents the ultimate end of society, which is ordered to him" (§1929).

"The duty of making oneself a neighbor to others and actively serving them becomes even more urgent when it involves the disadvantaged, in whatever area this may be. 'As you did it to one of the least of these my brethren, you did it to me' " (Matt 25:40 quoted in §1932).

"There also exist sinful inequalities that affect millions of men and women. These are in open contradiction of the Gospel" (§1938).

"The principle of solidarity, also articulated in terms of 'friendship' or 'social charity,' is a direct demand of human and Christian brotherhood" (§1939).

"Solidarity is manifested in the first place by distribution of goods and remuneration for work. It also presupposes the effort for a more just social order where tensions are better able to be reduced and conflicts more readily settled by negotiation" (§1940).

"Socioeconomic problems can be resolved only with the help of all the forms of solidarity: solidarity of the poor among themselves, between rich and poor, of workers among themselves, between employers and employees in business, solidarity among nations and peoples. International solidarity is a requirement of the moral order; world peace in part depends upon this" (§1941).

"The equal dignity of human persons requires the effort to reduce excessive social and economic inequalities" (§1947).

is the sullen reply. He sees another slathering cement on bricks. The man asks what he is doing. "I'm laying bricks," he replies. The man asks a third guy who is lugging materials from one spot to another what he is doing. He smiles and says, "I'm building a cathedral." The cathedrals we build are not made of brick and mortar alone. Our real, lived experience of church rests on the images and meanings we bring to, and understandings we have of, the practices of our faith. St. Lawrence, a martyred deacon of the third century, when told by a Roman prefect to hand over the treasures and riches of the church, presented the poor and lame members of the community and said, "Here are the treasures of the Church."

The poor and marginalized have a special claim on our resources and affections when we profess to be living as members of the Catholic community. The person who has nothing is as much a member of our community as the one who has billions of dollars. Maybe more so. Novelist James Lee Burke, whose crime and mystery novels are filled with subtle Catholic themes and ideas, describes a sheriff in Texas being awakened in the middle of the night as Mexicans migrate into the United States. When did we become so afraid of a man with a hole in his shoe?

At 2:41 Saturday morning his head jerked up from his chest. Outside, he heard a heavy rock bounce down the arroyo, the breaking of a branch, a whisper of voices, then the sound of feet moving along the base of the hill. He unsnapped the strap on his revolver and got up from his desk and went to the back door. A dozen or more people were following his fence line towards his north pasture. One woman was carrying a suitcase and clutching an infant against her shoulder. The men were all short and wore baseball caps and multiple shirts and, in the moonlight, had the snubbed profiles of figures on Mayan sculptures. So these where the people who had been made into the new enemy, Hackberry thought. Campesinos, who sometimes had to drink one another's urine to survive in the desert. They were hungry, frightened, in total thrall to the coyotes who led them across, their only immediate goal a place where they could light a fire and cook their food without being seen. But as John Steinbeck had said long ago, we had come to fear a man with a hole in his shoe. (Burke 2011, 58)

At best, Jesuit schools challenge students to become aware of and aid those with holes in their shoes. Jesuit Mark Ravizza works with the *Casa de la Solidaridad* in El Salvador, a program for students from Jesuit Universities in the United States engaged in a study abroad–service learning experience. Students go to El Salvador for a full semester during which they take two days a week to engage in working with organizations and people serving the community at "praxis sites." Students take courses, engage in theological and social reflection on their work and experiences in El Salvador, and are challenged to engage in their own personal formation in the context of community. Weekly spirituality nights and regular community practices of sharing everything from house chores to prayer help integrate what they learn and experience while in Central America (Ravizza in Rausch 2010, 112-13). Those of us who work with students often urge this kind of reflection with catchphrases like, "Don't have the experience and miss the meaning." Fourteen weeks spent on site, along with the built-in reflection, makes it difficult to miss the meaning.

The most important and impactful aspects of the Casa program are the ways in which the students share life with the Salvadoran people. These communal realities burst into students' lives and consciousness in unexpected and startling moments. Mark shares the experience of community of one of the students, a young woman he calls Susan, who visits the home of a poor family. The mother of the house, named Oti, literally touched Susan in a way this young woman from the United States will remember forever. The day before, Susan had been bitten by bugs, and her legs began to itch around the "swollen, red bug bites."

She told me she had a little medicine, a 'special ointment,' that she had been saving. . . . [She] returned with a small tube of cream, half full. I put out my hand expecting that she would give me a bit of the lotion to put on my legs. But instead, Oti squeezed the entire tube into her own hands, and then got down on her knees and began to massage the cream gently into my burning skin. (Ravizza 2010, 113)

Susan reflects and wonders why she assumed that Oti would simply squeeze some ointment in her hand.

And why, instead, did she put everything she had into her own hands, and lavish it so generously on me? The cream was a gift she'd been saving for months. She doesn't have the money to buy more. I didn't deserve it or have any right to it, and yet for Oti this was the only natural thing to do. Why do I see the world so differently than she does? (Ravizza 2010, 114)

I too have been privileged to be taught about community by the generosity of someone I met in a land far from where I was born—a Chilean woman who gave me a simple, extraordinary meal, a feast I've never forgotten. It was a cold and rainy night in Osorno, deep in southern Chile in the early 1980s. The Chilean middle class was suffering from horrific economic downturns. The poor had always felt the downside of supply-side economic policies, but many more in the country were metaphorically wet and cold in new and unexpected ways. I was grateful for the parka the Jesuit community had gotten for me which kept me warm and dry in the Osorno rains. But what really warmed me in Chile was the constant welcome and generosity of the Chilean people.

"Hola, Ricardito," called out the parents of a San Mateo student as they drove by. They opened the door of their car. "Ven. Te invitamos a nuestra casa." Soon, I was comfortable and dry in a small, middle-class home, the wood fire glowing and warming the kitchen. The lady of the house was preparing an evening meal of fried eggs and mashed potatoes.

To tell the truth, I wasn't a big fan of the way Chileans prepared eggs, floating the egg on two inches of hot cooking oil. It made for a greasy lump on top of the mashed potatoes. Still, I didn't want to seem ungrateful, and I thanked her as she laid plates with a baseball-size mound of potatoes and one egg in front of her husband and the same baseball size mound of potatoes and one egg in front of me. Then she sat down and announced, "Yo, no tengo hambre" (I'm not hungry").

As I lifted my fork, it dawned on me. It was a bit of a shock to realize there were only two eggs in the house. She served her husband one. She gave the other one to me. She had given me her dinner. I ate slowly and thoughtfully. I had been taught that it would be an insult to refuse the generosity of the Chileans.

I've never forgotten that simple, extraordinary meal.

That night I realized this lovely, generous Chilean woman, in a country famous for hospitality to the stranger in their midst, had given me her food and gone hungry. I was, and still am, humbled and in awe of her way of being, a "*modo de ser*" that taught me much about Chilean culture, about how to treat others, about how to be like Christ, and about the message and challenge of the Eucharist.

Many Jesuits in lands far from where they were born have learned similar lessons about community. The irrepressible Don Ward, S.J., who has spent many years in Africa and Chile, once said, "Sandra, the head of the English department in Chile, taught me ever so slowly and gently that to belong to a family, far from being a limitation—it did not mean blood or language or culture—is an expansion of all of one's preconceived notions" (Ward 2009).

Community is the life blood and massive meaning of Catholicism. Our Catholic imagination concerning community expands and extends to those of other faith traditions and communities. At the University of Scranton, during our large public ceremonies, I will often lead prayer and invite all to pray "in the faith tradition in which you root your soul." At graduation, I will quote the Hebrew Scriptures and the Qur'an. Given the generosity of the Jewish community to the university, and the relatively large number of Muslims who attend our business school, it is only fitting to do so. Such openness and universality should characterize our pastoral practice and imaginations. And our communal imagination should always have a privileged space for the poor.

Pope John Paul II prophetically proclaims that we need:

> to face squarely the reality of an innumerable multitude of people—children, adults and the elderly—in other words, real and unique human persons, who are suffering under the intolerable burden of poverty. There are many millions who are deprived of hope due to the fact that, in many parts of the world, their situation has noticeably worsened. Before these tragedies of total indigence and need, in which so many of our brothers and sisters are living, it is the Lord Jesus himself who comes to question us (cf. Mt 25:31-46). (John Paul II, *On Social Concern*, §13).

We find God in and through our experience of community. We find God in and through realizing that the whole human family is our family, our community. That is the great meaning of the Eucharist. This is the meaning of church. Gerard Manley Hopkins says it best.

> I say more: the just man justices;
> Keeps grace: that keeps all his goings graces;
> Acts in God's eye what in God's eye he is—
> Christ—for Christ plays in ten thousand places,
> Lovely in limbs, and lovely in eyes not his
> To the Father through the features of men's faces.

CHAPTER 5

The Church: Both Divine and Human

. . . the people of God, or the church, is the sacrament of the reign of God in the process of becoming reality.
—Lohfink, *Jesus of Nazareth*, 56

Those who are more influential because they have greater share of goods and common services should feel responsible for the weaker and be ready to share with them all they possess. . . . the church feels called to take her stand beside the poor, to discern the justice of their requests and to help satisfy them, without losing sight of the good of groups in the context of the common good.
—John Paul II, *On Social Concern* §39

There's an old joke about a department store with a magic elevator that will take women to a floor where they can meet certain kinds of men. The rule, though, is that the elevator goes up, but if you pass that floor, you can't go back down again. On floor 1 the door opens and there's a sign saying, "Men here are nice guys. If you ascend higher, you cannot return to this floor." On floor 2, the door opens and there's a sign saying, "Men here are nice guys and have a job. If you ascend higher, you cannot return to this floor." The third floor has a sign, "Men here are nice guys, have a job, and like kids. If you ascend higher, you cannot return to this floor." On the fourth floor the sign reads, "Men here are nice guys, have a job, like kids, and clean and cook. If you ascend higher, you cannot return to this floor." On the fifth floor the sign says, "Men here are nice guys, have a job, like kids, like to clean and cook, and really listen to you. If you ascend higher, you cannot return to this floor." On the sixth floor the door opens and a large sign announces, "If you've come this far, it's clear you can never be satisfied."

OK, I apologize for the sexist tone of the joke. It can certainly be told the other way around, I'm sure. The point is that so many people want a church that not only doesn't exist but could never exist. The church, like everything else, is a social structure and an all-too-human community. The church is a hospital for sinners, not a showcase for saints. I think one of the really powerful aspects of the old practice of confessions on Saturday afternoons at the parish was "the lines." When we walked into the church, the fact that we saw, physically present, others like ourselves, in line, waiting there to confess their failures and shortcomings, we knew we weren't the only ones who didn't have our act together. The physical presence of others sent a subliminal message that we're all incomplete, that we all need the forgiveness and mercy of God and one another. It doesn't seem to me that one-on-one confession, by appointment, with the priest carries the same tone or feel. It's more like a session with a therapist than a community together asking for and receiving forgiveness. Communal reconciliation services, with the opportunity for individual confessions, seem to me a better option. We all need help and healing.

The guy who started "Write Love On Your Arms" came to the University of Scranton and spoke to five hundred undergrad students. His message of hope and healing was mesmerizing to this emergent adult audience. During his talk, I saw only a few students pulling out their cell phones to text someone. What struck me was his assumption that virtually all the young people in the room were struggling with the pain of isolation, the fear of letting others know who they really are, the worry that there is something horrible that will befall one as a matter of course.

The church should be an institution set up to address people's pain and confusion. Jesus wants us to change how we relate to one another. Too often what seems to preoccupy us professional church people (liturgical niceties, canon law concerning marriage, fund-raising) is far from the real spiritual, emotional, and physical needs of God's people in a whirlwind world.

The job description of priests ought to have a line in it that instructs those of us privileged to be ordained for the service of God's people (not "our" people, or "my" people) that we should spend at least one day a week steering toward the pain in people's lives and society's structures. But too often seminaries are preparing priests to be anything but agents of transformative love and healing hope. Priests are being taught to answer questions people are no longer asking. Too often, priests see their role as "dispensing" sacraments, rather than making the community a sacrament of reconciliation, peace, justice, and love.

What frustrates our ability to be the church God wants and needs is our own bitter and deep-seated divisions and frozen mind-sets. The never-ending painful polarization between those some call conservative and those some call liberal is confusing and painful for those caught in the middle, especially when people come and complain about someone ostentatiously throwing themselves on their knees to receive communion or about how teenagers are dressed in church. If not rooted in one or the other camp, priests and other church ministers get caught in the crossfire of these groups' bullets shooting at one another. Sometimes I think that when we are ordained they should just tie ropes to our wrists and let the people pull.

But they make us lie on the floor. Those who lie on the ground get walked on and over. One profound piece of advice I got before I was ordained was from a sister from a religious order. She told those of us preparing for ordination, "Remember. Feel the floor." The church doesn't exist for the priests. We are not the most important people in the congregation. We are not special. Priests are to serve the people of God. Especially in the wake of the scandal, we have to earn our collars every day.

The scandal: Given the revelations of priests' sexual abuse of minors, all Catholics are challenged to try to comprehend the whole tragic morass surrounding clerical sex abuse that has been revealed in the past decade. Let us pray for and support victims, try to understand all involved, and strive to construct a church wherein sexual abuse of children never happens again.

Fools rush in where angels fear to tread. Well, no one ever called me an angel. And it may be foolish to try to say anything in the today's context that simply doesn't echo the endless charges of "cover-up," "insensitive/incompetent/criminal bishops," or "the church still doesn't 'get it.'" Yet I hope thinking through the crisis will be more helpful than self-righteously and loudly condemning the hierarchy.

First, know that I, and any sane and sensitive priest, hate and abhor what was done by priests to innocent children. One child molested is one too many. The pedophiles and ephebophiles in the church have caused incalculable harm to both the children they abused and violated, and all those torn apart by collateral damage. SNAP (Survivors Network of those Abused by Priests) and other organizations deserve our thanks for forcing all to deal with these realities.

In 1985, as the disturbing reports of serial child molester Fr. Gilbert Gauthe of Louisiana became known, due in large part to the courageous journalism of Jason Berry and the *National Catholic Reporter,* I was in theology studies. Those were turbulent times for those preparing for ordination. Liberation theology and questions such as women's ordination were being hotly debated. Gauthe's case raised even more questions. Those of us who were given the grace to persevere to ordination knew we were in for a rough ride. Little did we know.

After ordination in 1988, I was sent to our Jesuit parish in Camden, New Jersey. Early in his tenure, Bishop James T. McHugh called all the priests working in the Camden diocese to a mandatory meeting. He let it be known in no uncertain terms: things were changing. We were told if there was an accusation against any of us, we were on our own. Prepare to get a lawyer. Do not expect any preferential treatment from the diocese. Civil authorities would be informed. I was impressed. I thought, "Good. This is being handled. Cases like Gauthe's won't happen again."

Was I wrong. The efforts of bishops like McHugh were too little, too late. The 2002-2003 daily front page excoriations of the church burst the festering boil. Under mounting pressure, the bishops autho-rized an independent study. The John Jay College of Criminal Justice found that between 1950 and 2002, 4 percent of Catholic priests had been accused of sexual abuse. 10,667 people reported being sexually abused as children by 4,392 priests, about 4 percent of all 109,694 priests (USCCB 2011, 8). The study also found that the rate of pedophilia in the church was no higher than in other institutions in society. The sad case of Jerry Sandusky at Penn State revealed that many other institutions and revered figures like Coach Joe Paterno acted much the way Catholic bishops too often did. And the church, far from covering up, had reams of documentation about these cases. Many other institutions keep no records at all. If someone complains to a public school district they may well hear, "You're asking about Mr. Jones who taught second grade in 1979? Don't know what hap-pened to him."

I don't blame the media for focusing attention on the crimes, but when *ABC Evening News* reports (03/29/10), relying on www.bishopsaccountability.org, that 5 to 10 percent of priests "are abus-ers," they contradict the most authoritative study done on the issue. Still, the 96 percent of priests, the 99.9 percent of sisters, and the vast majority of the laity who never hurt a child also have had to confront what all this means.

Newsweek reported in April 2010 that Catholic priests' rate of abusing children is no more than other institutions:

> Experts who study child abuse say they see little reason to con-clude that sexual abuse is mostly a Catholic issue. "We don't see the Catholic Church as a hotbed of this or a place that has a bigger problem than anyone else," said Ernie Allen, president of the National Center for Missing and Exploited Children. "I can tell you without hesitation that we have seen cases in many religious settings, from traveling evangelists to mainstream ministers to rabbis and others." (Wingert 2010).

The problem is massive and extends far beyond the church's walls: 25 percent of girls and 16 percent of boys will be sexually abused before their eighteenth birthday, and 20 percent of all children will suffer abuse before the age of eight. There are thirty-nine million people in the United States today who have survived sexual abuse in their childhood. 30 to 40 percent suffer abuse at the hands of a family member or an older child. Only 10 percent are abused by strangers (http://www.darkness2light. org/KnowAbout/statistics_2.asp).

To understand what happened, one must realize this: what previously had been considered a sin came to be understood as a crime. What once was seen as a treatable, compulsive condition, understood as something to be handled quietly by an institution's authorities, came to be seen as something best dealt with by the criminal justice system, with the full light of the mass media shining on the proceedings. Cultural mores shifted, obviously for the better. Back when homosexual activity was considered a crime, pedophilia (Andrew Sullivan and others call it "child rape") committed by a priest was a sin. In the 1960s and 1970s, police were routinely sent out to try to catch homosexuals in the act and arrest them. Today homosexuality is accepted by large sectors of society. Several years ago the military dropped their "Don't ask, don't tell" policy, and several states now allow same-sex marriage. In contrast, priest pedophiles are those who can never be understood, nor forgiven, and any bishop that didn't defrock a priest after the first allegation is considered guilty of a cover-up.

Priests who abuse children today are justly treated as criminals. Their pedophiliac condition, whether caused by their being molested as children themselves, or perversely freely chosen, results in arrest and jail time. The children molested by priests can sue the church, a possibility denied many children molested by adults in other institutions. Statute-of-limitation laws are overridden, and the criminal justice system yields to cries for vengeance, or justice, depending on your perspective. The reason given: many so traumatized cannot come forward in the time allotted. The church has paid billions, and the bills keep piling up. Much of the money comes from people in the pews who did no wrong. Millions go to lawyers, who are not working pro bono.

The constantly repeated charge of cover-up masks the fact that many bishops and religious superiors were following the standard operating procedures of the times. In 1961, John Fitzgerald Kennedy, a Catholic, had to justify his right to run for president. In that year, if a Bishop McGillicuddy had taken a Fr. Smith down to the local precinct and told the police sergeant to book him, and that Johnny the altar boy would soon be brought in by his parents to press charges, everyone would have said the bishop was crazy. In 1952, 1966, 1974, or 1982, neither parents nor police were publicly decrying how bishops handled these matters. In those times, if journalists knew about it, they weren't saying any more than they did about John Kennedy's multiple marital infidelities. Often money was given either to pay for needed therapy for the victim or, in some small measure, to try to make amends. Now such payments are categorized as "hush money." Rene Girard's cogent analysis of scapegoating is applicable here. We need someone to blame, someone to punish: bishops are the most convenient target.

Well into the late 1980s, church leaders were being told by therapists at rehab centers that priests with this "problem" had been "treated" and could be placed back in ministerial positions, sometimes with the caveat that the priest would have no contact with minors. What seems so horrible now, the moving of priests from parish to parish, did not seem so crazy in 1978. That was the year the North American Man/Boy Love Association (NAMBLA) was formed. It is incredible that that organization still exists and has a website, but in 1978 it seems their views were worth at least being given a hearing. To think or speak as if this problem exists in the Catholic Church alone is disingenuous. Again, just google "Penn State, Joe Paterno and Jerry Sandusky." Experts opine that 10 to 20 percent of males in the United States abuse sexually (Wingert 2010).

It was not the fact of the matter that bishops were sitting around conspiring to actively encourage priests to go and molest more children. Bishops, parents, police, and everyone else in the decades preceding the sexual revolution of the late 1960s did not deal openly or forthrightly with sexual matters. Bishops probably wanted to handle these matters quickly and quietly and get on to other concerns. Does this indicate (1) a "cover-up" evidencing a callous disregard for the welfare of children, (2) a justifiable fear of gravely harming the church by being open about this issue, or (3) in hindsight, bewildering incompetence? Probably a combination of the second (and in their defense, note how these revelations have hurt the church) and third (no one suggests the bishops did anything right). Still, I hesitate to charge them with the first.

The vast majority of bishops were good and decent men, and none of them had any training, nor much help, in dealing with sexual deviants. Nor were they schooled in the intricacies of public relations in a world with a 24/7 news cycle. A Jesuit would get appointed provincial and in a matter of weeks go from decades of scholarly pursuits to a six-year term as an administrator of some six hundred to one thousand men, without a day of management training. The bishops cared deeply about children, but what could we expect them to have done, given the times and cultural cues available to them? They didn't act any differently than the family who kept a close eye on Uncle Eddie at Thanksgiving or the school principal who kept Mr. Jones away from the first and second graders. If the bishops and provincials had covered this up, there would not be hundreds of thousands of incriminating letters and other documents in church files.

Even parents were not always immediately outraged. Even parents did not initially call for priests to be put in jail. The first reaction to Gauthe was to get him "help." In 1972, Gauthe was caught after molesting three boys. Parents confronted him. In his deposition Gauthe stated, "They simply asked me if I had been involved with any of the children, and I said, 'Yes.' And I asked them if they would help me find a good psychiatrist." A lady made an appointment for him. "And," he said, "I simply kept it." Gauthe said the parents paid for these sessions, which lasted several months and that he did not report them to Church superiors (http://www.bishop-accountability.org/news/1985_05_23_Berry_TheTragedy.htm).

In the 1980s, a Jesuit in California moved to Los Angeles, where he was able to visit his brother and his family more easily and more often. He was caught molesting his nieces by his brother, an LAPD officer. His brother, a cop, didn't arrest him. He told him he needed to get help. "I threw him out of my house," Larry Lindner said. He urged his brother to seek treatment but did not report him to authorities. "I trusted him," Larry Lindner said. "I told him, 'I'm not going to ruin your life or ruin your career. Just go get help.' . . . I should have had him arrested right there. But he's still my brother, and I did what I thought a brother should do" (http://www.bishop-accountability. org/news5/2002_12_14_Bunting_LAPriest.htm).

Many bishops who acted like those parents in the Gauthe case or Officer Lindner are being castigated for not acting as omniscient CEOs. In reality, the relationship of bishop to priest ought to be more like brother to brother than boss to employee. The bishops had to consider and care for all the church: the victims, the victimizers, and everyone else who would be affected by revelations of abuse.

In 1990, a good and balanced movie, *Judgment*, starring Keith Carradine and Blythe Danner, presented the excruciatingly difficult choices bishops confronted. In one scene, the bishop wants to reach out pastorally to the family of children abused by a priest character based on the real life Gilbert Gauthe. The lawyers tell the bishop if he meets with the family he will be admitting guilt. He is told he can speak with the family or save the diocese from financial ruin. But he cannot do both.

In the age before Oprah and reality TV's constant self-revelation, the world and church felt that some things were not aired in public, much the way universities don't place date rape info in their recruitment materials, nor do banks highlight the history of any embezzlers in their midst. Today, some bishops are unjustly held to a standard neither they, nor anyone else at the time, expected them to meet. Many of those bishops are dead. Many who were bishops and provincials in the 1980s gradually began to realize a radically different approach was needed, thanks to their heeding voices like Fr. Andrew Greeley's and Fr. Tom Doyle's. But, frankly, giving a position of authority and power to Bishop Bernard F. Law, who continued old practices well beyond the time that things had changed, is insane and disgraceful.

Since 2002, the church has had a policy of zero tolerance. If anyone accuses a priest, the priest is immediately removed from ministry until the matter is resolved. Although false accusations are rare, priests are completely vulnerable to whoever wants to make a baseless claim. Priests must never engage in any kind of abuse. The church's Essential Norms document states: "When even a single act of sexual abuse by a priest or deacon is admitted or is established after an appropriate process in accord with canon law, the offending priest or deacon will be removed permanently from ecclesiastical ministry, not excluding dismissal from the clerical state, if the case so warrants" (USCCB 2005-2006, norm #8)."

The problem isn't zero tolerance. The problem isn't celibacy—96 percent of the priests were not pedophiles, while many married men are. The problem isn't homosexuality. The investigators from the John Jay College of Criminal Justice told the bishops in 2011 that there is no connection between homosexual priests and pedophilia (USCCB 2011). The high incidence of boys being molested by priests was due to the fact that priests had easier access to boys. Fr. Bill taking the altar boys on a camping trip was considered wonderful for the boys and he was considered a "great guy." If Fr. Bill had suggested taking the fifth and sixth grade girls on a camping trip, people would have thought that weird. The problem isn't callous and insensitive bishops or incompetent provincials. Most of them did the best they could with the resources and within the cultural mores available at the time. The problem is what do we do now and in the future?

The amazing reality is that so many Catholics are sticking with the church. Recently, I presided at a First Communion celebration. A packed church accompanying some forty second graders, the boys looking cool in blue suits and the girls in an array of white dresses, the parents hovering as they walk up with their child to receive the Lord in the Eucharist, along with the grandparents, brothers and sisters, the teachers and the school's big kids in the choir and acting as altar servers: the church continues.

We need new Catherines of Siena, Francises of Assisi, Ignatiuses of Loyola, John Paul IIs, Dorothy Days, Thomas Mertons, Óscar

Romeros and Daniel Berrigans to reinvigorate and renew the church. The Catholic Church is the largest private provider of social services in the United States. We cannot allow Catholic schools, soup kitchens, nursing homes, hospitals, social outreach, family service organizations, immigration services, prison ministries, AIDS ministries, and myriad other local, national, and global charitable institutions to fall victim to the present crisis.

The thousands of children harmed can never be forgotten or ignored. But let's not compound the crimes of a small percentage of priests by letting their actions destroy not just the souls and lives of too many children but also the mission and ministries of the whole church.

In 1975 the Society of Jesus defined the Jesuit mission as "The service of faith of which the promotion of Justice is an absolute requirement. For reconciliation with God demands the reconciliation of people with one another" (32nd General Congregation, 1975). Many quickly picked up on the phrase "faith and justice" or the "faith that does justice." But the reconciliation theme dropped out and received much less attention.

Today, and at all times, we need to do justice and work toward reconciliation. How to reconcile over the issues of how the sexual abuse of children was addressed by the church as an institution, how to find some way to get to forgiveness—these are huge challenges for us as the pilgrim people of God, as the Body of Christ. Yet these are challenges we must meet. Issues such as abortion, the use of artificial means of birth control, homosexuality and same-sex marriage, on and on, call us to be agents of reconciliation. Genocides, economic inequality, and pollution of the planet call us to be agents of reconciliation.

One area that pains and confuses many is not only the church's refusal to ordain women but the official stance that we are not even to speak of it. Some say the issue has been decided and will never be changed (again, think of the church's never-changing teachings on usury, slavery, and salvation outside the church). But half the human race is female, and many—both male and female—want an answer as to why we cannot even speak of women being priests. Still, no matter where you stand on the issue, the truth is that the church needs priests, good and holy priests. But being a priest does not make one a better Catholic than those not ordained. We all share in the one priesthood of Jesus Christ. We are all called to be a priestly and prophetic people.

On a Holy Thursday at Holy Name Parish in Camden, I wanted to get across the idea that we are all called to be priestly and prophetic people. Here I translate what I originally wrote in Spanish. As Sr. Linda interpretively danced, we told this story to get the point across.

> *Once upon a time, there was a people in darkness (TURN OFF THE LIGHTS IN THE CHURCH).*
>
> *This people suffered the pain of the lack of light, the lack of education, the lack of love, the lack of hope, the lack of peace, the lack of justice, the lack of faith. The people had forgotten how to love one another, how to serve one another, how to trust, how to pardon those who trespass against us. The people needed the Light to open their eyes and see the presence of God in their midst. The people desired to receive the power of God to transform the situation. The people needed the liberation that God offers, but the people weren't able to see this liberation because the people were in darkness.*
>
> *There was once a priestly person, a person baptized for the community, baptized in the light of Christ, enlightened by the light of the Gospel, confirmed in the mission of the community. This priestly person participated frequently in the celebration of the Eucharist, at the table of the Lord, the Holy Mass. This priestly person saw the suffering of the people. She decided to give testimony of the truth of God, the Good News of Jesus Christ. She began to share the light (SR. LINDA STARTS LIGHTING EVERYONE'S HAND-HELD CANDLES). She was carrying the light to and for all the people.*
>
> *She went among all the people carrying the light that had been trapped in the darkness. Light in the darkness, light where there*

only existed the night without day. She went among all the people giving the light of Christ.

Where there had been darkness, she brought light. Where there was darkness she began to radiate light, with brightness and warmth. Where there was a lack of peace, this priestly person carried the Word of God, consoling, confirming, and offering a challenge. Where there had been a lack of pardon, this priestly person went among the people reconciling one with another, persons with their families, communities with other communities, all peoples with God.

Where there had been a lack of trust, the priestly person went about speaking, pushing, and animating the people. Where there had been oppression, oppression of the poor by the rich, oppression of the community by those who buy and sell illegal drugs, oppression of women by men, the priestly person spoke the truth of the Gospel, calling all the people to justice, to truth, to peace. Where there had been hate and the desire for revenge, the priestly person shared the light of the presence of God, the power of transformation, the power to change the way of being of the people.

With the light of Christ shining in the community, the young people began to learn how to be persons, liberated persons, capable and with confidence in themselves. With the light of Christ the people began to walk toward justice, toward peace, toward love. With the light, the elderly were able to enjoy their golden years content, in peace and tranquility. With the light, the people were able to live as daughters and sons of God. The light revealed the presence of God deep within the people, among brothers and sisters.

The priestly person now disappeared among the people. Now she was no longer known as the priestly person because the people had become a priestly people. All the people now did the things that she had done. All the darkness disappeared, and the light of Christ guided the people along the Way.

One of the main obstacles to our becoming a truly priestly people is the deep and dangerous divisions that have characterized the church in recent decades. In my previous book, *A Faith That Frees* (Orbis, 2008), I argued that the real problems in the church are not theological but cultural. We have at least two cultural currents flowing in the church in the United States in the wake of Vatican II. Call the currents "liberal" and "conservative," "kingdom Catholics" and "communion Catholics," "left" or "right"—all the bickering and backstabbing comes down to a frightening loss of energy and enthusiasm among those committed to trying to live the Catholic way of life, and bewilderment to those wondering why to join, or remain with, such a contentious crowd. Add in the clerical sex abuse scandals and you have a recipe for disaster.

Let's call the currents "Purple" and "Violet," because in many ways they are similar. The problem is, we too often accentuate differences rather than celebrate similarities. Let me give a representative "lineup" of the two "teams" and some of their emphases.

Purple team	*Violet team*
Karl Rahner, S.J.	Pope Benedict XVI (Joseph Ratzinger)
St . Thomas Aquinas	St. Augustine
Gaudium et Spes	*Lumen Gentium*
Kingdom Catholics	Communion Catholics
Starts with human experience	Starts with revelation
God- and world-centered	Christ- and church-centered
We discover truth in dialogue	We dialogue to tell the truth
Joan Chittister, OSB, Margaret Farley, RSM	Mother Angelica, Nashville Dominicans
Simone Campbell & Nuns on the Bus	Elizabeth Scalia, the Anchoress
Jesuit universities	Cardinal Newman Society
John Dear, S.J.	Joe Fessio, S.J.
Orbis Books	Ignatius Press
Liberation theology	Theology of the Body
National Catholic Reporter	*National Catholic Register*
Nancy Pelosi, Joe Biden	Rick Santorum, Newt Gingrich

Both teams are good and needed in the church today, although the Violets are much more likely to suggest that the Purples just leave. The real disgrace of the tensions and polarizations of the past thirty or forty years is that the vast majority of younger Catholics have little awareness of, or interest in, the battles these two camps have engaged in over the past decades. Most young women at Jesuit universities have little interest in the women's ordination issue (which pleases the Violets) while even fewer have any interest at all in becoming a sister in religious life (which should challenge the Purples). Many younger Catholics in the Violet circles have little awareness of Catholic social teaching, while their counterparts in the Purple arenas have not heard of eucharistic adoration or Gregorian chant. I was giving a talk to a large group of mostly recent college grads who were going off to give services as Jesuit International Volunteers and other Catholic organizations, and one young man said he'd never even heard of EWTN, the Catholic channel that is decidedly Violet and has become the face of the Catholic community for many in the United States. Why the Purples won't get it together and produce television programming baffles me.

Both currents are legitimate. They both play sports, but one plays football and the other baseball. When the football team asks the baseball players how many touchdowns they scored, the question does not compute. When the baseball players ask the football players how many home runs they've hit, the same incomprehension ensues.

Wherever you stand on this ideological spectrum, one thing is certain. Millions are confused, hurt, and frustrated by the constant tension and arguments over things like receiving communion in the hand or on the tongue. Refusing to allow girls to be altar servers seems not only repugnant and exceedingly sexist to many; it flies in the face of the reality of the vast majority of the parishes allowing girls to serve at the altar (many priests note that the girls are more conscientious and responsible than the boys). One diocese allows an exemption from the abstinence from meat when St. Patrick's Day falls on a Friday in Lent. The diocese across the river refuses to allow the exemption. One diocese in Nebraska excommunicates members of the long-standing liberal church group Call to Action. When asked if the adjacent diocese will also excommunicate the group, questioners are met by silence. Such contradictory policies leave normal people scratching their heads wondering what is up with that crazy Catholic Church? All this polarization has resulted in what I have called in my previous book "meaning meltdown" and a great diminishment of the church in myriad ways. The headline for John Allen's story in the *National Catholic Reporter* reads, "Right wing 'generally not happy' with Francis, Chaput says" (Allen 2013). The pope has Mass with four million young folks in Brazil at World Youth Day, and a week later all a prominent archbishop can opine in response is that the "right wing" of the church is unhappy. Such dissension does not build up the Body of Christ.

Charles Taylor in his comprehensive, complex, and penetrating analysis of our times, *A Secular Age*, traces the depths and history of the battles between those who want the church to stand in opposition to the changing of the tradition(s) begun at Trent and those who want to support the winds of change brought in by Vatican II. "What is the right understanding of Catholic Christianity? . . . Then the issue is, who got it right, Vatican II or Trent, and/or in which respect?" (Taylor 2007, 752).

What many fail to understand is that the halcyon days of yore simply do not exist. The notion that in the past religious practice was so much more fervent and consistent doesn't hold up to scrutiny. Historian Molly Worthen reveals:

> The truth is that "nones" are nothing new. Religion has been a feature of human society since Neanderthal times, but so has religious indifference. Our illusions of the past as a golden age of faith tend to cloud our assessment of today's religious landscape. We think of atheism and religious apathy as uniquely modern spiritual options, ideas that Voltaire and Hume devised in a coffee house one rainy afternoon sometime in the 18th century. Before the Enlightenment, legend has it, peasants hurried to church every week and princes bowed and scraped before priests.

Historians have yet to unearth Pew studies from the 13th century, but it is safe to say that we frequently overestimate medieval piety. Ordinary people often skipped church and had a feeble grasp of basic Christian dogma. Many priests barely understood the Latin they chanted—and many parishes lacked any priest at all. Bishops complained about towns that used their cathedrals mainly as indoor markets or granaries. Lest Protestants blame this irreverence on Catholic corruption, the evidence suggests that it continued after Martin Luther nailed his theses to the Wittenberg church door. In 1584, census takers in Antwerp discovered that the city had a larger proportion of "nones" than twenty-first-century America: a full third of residents claimed no religious affiliation. (Worthen 2012)

Still, often cited statistics reveal a disturbing decline in church attendance and participation since the 1950s. In the United States, one of every three persons raised Catholic no longer considers himself or herself to be a member of the church. That makes former Catholics the second largest religious group in the country (Pew Forum 2008). CARA (Center for Applied Research in the Apostolate) reports that only 15 percent of young Catholics (ages eighteen to twenty-nine) attend Mass weekly.

It is time to get back to basics, to sharing the good news and how to live the message in loving service of one another. God doesn't care if you ring bells at the consecration or not. God does care if our celebration of the Eucharist is transforming us into a priestly people, a prophetic people, a people on fire with the energy and wisdom and courage of the Holy Spirit. It is time to work together and not against one another.

Everyone has a place at the table in God's kingdom. Our church should be no different. Let us welcome one another, rather than castigate and judge one another. Tom Clifford, S.J., once voiced a cogent question to ask ourselves when we think someone in community is off base: "Is what he is doing really wrong, or is it that I just don't like it?" Let's start working together for God's people and the salvation of the world.

A crew team made up of Jesuits couldn't get their boat moving in the right direction, let alone moving fast. Every day they'd struggle to get into the boat. If they didn't capsize it, they'd still only get it going in circles. So they finally sent one of their Jesuit crew team members over to spy on what the Sisters of Mercy crew team was doing on a nearby lake. He cames back and told his fellow Jesuits, "We're doing it all wrong. The sisters have the secret." The Jesuits ask him, "What is it?" "They have eight rowing and only one yelling!" Let's stop yelling and grab an oar.

CHAPTER 6

Righting Relationships: The Work of Justice and Forgiveness

Jesus was not just concerned with souls. He wanted a changed society.

—Lohfink, *Jesus of Nazareth*, 52

Sin is present in human history; any attempt to ignore it or to give this dark reality other names would be futile. To try and understand what sin is, one must first recognize the profound relation of man to God, for only in this relationship is the evil of sin unmasked in its true identity as humanity's rejection of God . . . even as it continues to weigh heavy on human life and history.

—CCC §386

You are not making a gift of your possessions to the poor person. You are handing over to him what is his. For what you have been given in common for the use of all, you have arrogated to yourself. The world is given to all, and not only to the rich.

— St. Ambrose

The way society responds to the needs of the poor through its public policies is the litmus test of its justice or injustice.

—USCCB, "Economic Justice for All," §123

The second-grade teacher has to step out of class for a moment and she tells all the children to behave until she returns. Five minutes later, as she turns the corner onto her corridor, the teacher hears the predictable yells and noise of twenty-five seven-year-olds having a little too much fun. Little Mary was standing outside the classroom door. "What's the matter, Mary?" the teacher asks. "Why are you standing out here in the hall?" Mary replies with a mixture of frustration and annoyance, "We're all being bad and we don't know how to stop."

We're being bad, and we don't know how to stop. An apt description of the human condition. St. Paul describes the reality well: "For I do not do the good I want, but the evil I do not want is what I do" (Rom 7:15). Original sin, the doctrine that states that things are not the way they ought to be, is the only teaching for which we have empirical evidence. Just turn on the evening news, or look in a mirror. Sin is the condition, choice, and consequence of our being out of sorts with our deepest, truest selves. Sin is both personal and social.

Sin is what messes up our lives. Often what we ourselves do messes up what we deeply, truly desire. That's personal sin (e.g., I cheat on my wife—think Tiger Woods). Often it is what others do that messes up our lives. That's social sin (e.g., large social dynamics that harm us all directly or indirectly—think corporations ruthlessly polluting the planet, or businesses underpaying workers and failing to provide health care). Sin destroys the good that ought to be present in a situation or a person. Sin separates us from God, others, and the person we want to be. Sin hurts us when we choose to sin, and when others choose to sin against us.

What if we get to heaven and Jesus has a wristband, WDYD (What Did You Do)? As those on fire with the love and power of the Holy Spirit, we are called to respond to sin and those who suffer sin. Our faith impels us to confront sin and injustice and make things right.

Betty (not her real name) was a bubbly, engaged, articulate, and happy undergrad at a Jesuit university. She was an officer in student government and a stellar student in her major in the helping professions. I met her many times and in many venues. She always had a smile, an effusive greeting, and a general air of the joy of life that radiates from young adults. On many college campuses, there is a ritual called Take Back the Night. It is an effort to raise the awareness of dating violence, rape, and other acts of violence against primarily women but also against all who are in a position of vulnerability before their attacker (e.g., children or employees). I marched with the crowd of three hundred down to the Town Square, where a stage and microphone had been set up. After some speakers, there was an open-mike session where victims of violence were encouraged to come forward and share their stories. Too often those who suffer such violence behind closed doors feel isolated and alone. There is healing strength in telling what happened to them in an affirmative, welcoming atmosphere. I stood, stunned, as Betty walked over to the microphone. She faced the crowd and began speaking. "I think I was four years old the first time I can remember my father picking me up and throwing me against the wall." She went on to share how her father abused her for years, repeatedly raping her when she was older.

My mother's half-sister was a college professor in mathematics who, at forty, had never married. At her parish on Long Island, she met a widower with five kids, ranging in age from five to twelve. Some family members wondered how she would react to such a drastic change in her life. But the marriage was wonderful. Family gatherings were enriched by all these new kids. And she and her husband had a child, Kevin. This boy was the pride and joy of everyone. He was funny and talented, and as a teenager became a terrific baseball player. By the time he was a sophomore in college, he had grown to be tall and handsome and personable. Even better, the epilepsy from which he had suffered as a youngster seemed to be totally under control. He had been able to obtain a driver's license, an indication that the epilepsy no longer seemed manifest in his life. Over Christmas break of his sophomore year of college, he was planning to go to Italy for the spring semester. One evening he went over to a friend's house, crashed there for the night as young people do, and died in his sleep of a grand mal seizure. At the time, I was shocked. Who dies of epilepsy? I found out such deaths are more common than I knew.

As I looked at Kevin in his coffin, I really had a go-round with God. As a priest in Camden, New Jersey, I had seen the death of dozens of young people, mostly young men caught up in the drug trade. Still, Kevin's death hit me hard. "Why God, why?" I asked. After several months of prayer and mud-wrestling with God, I came to the insight that I was assuming Kevin's life would have been wonderful. Maybe his early death saved him from trials and tribulations I couldn't imagine. Maybe he would have suffered from some painful and debilitating disease. Maybe his marriage would have been extremely painful. Maybe he would have been distracted for a second at the wheel and run over a child. Maybe God knows more than I.

Even if God knows more than we do, there is so much suffering and pain in our world. Young girls, like Betty, horrifically abused by their fathers. The Kevins of the world who die too young. Kids raped by their priests. Teenagers killed in car accidents. Parents declining as Alzheimer's disease robs them of memory and personality. On a perhaps less painful level, but often debilitating nevertheless, we feel that our lives never quite reached their potential. The opening for a promotion at our job never materializes or goes to someone just marginally better qualified or, worse, less qualified. The economy takes a bad turn and our pension or the worth of our house is halved. Physically we succumb to COPD (chronic obstructive pulmonary disease) or chronic arthritis or constant back pain. Life is full of pain and problems.

Pope John Paul II in his landmark encyclical *On Social Concern* articulates well the relationship between personal and social sin. He writes that "structures of sin," while growing from personal sins, snowball and thus become more difficult to eradicate on the personal level alone. "And thus they grow stronger, spread, and become the source of other sins, and so influence people's behavior." The pope notes, "'Sin' and 'structures of sin' are categories which are seldom applied to the situation of the contemporary world. However, one cannot easily gain a profound understanding of the reality that confronts us unless we give a name to the root of the evils which afflict us." He introduces the analysis of our human situation from the viewpoint of structures of sin or social sin, because he wants "to point out the true nature of the evil which faces us with respect to the development of peoples: it is a question of a moral evil, the fruit of many sins which lead to 'structures of sin.' To diagnose the evil in this way is to identify precisely, on the level of human conduct, the path to be followed in order to overcome it" (John Paul II, *On Social Concern* §§36-37).

In 2008, a Vatican bishop, Gianfranco Girotti, named seven social sins that characterize our age: (1) "bioethical" violations such as birth control, (2) "morally dubious" experiments such as stem cell research, (3) drug abuse, (4) polluting the environment, (5) contributing to widening divide between rich and poor, (6) excessive wealth, and (7) creating poverty (http://www.catholicnewsagency.com/news/vatican_ bishop_points_to_modern_social_sins/op).

One-third of our brothers and sisters on earth, some three billion people, live on less than $2.50 a day. 80 percent of the planet exists on less than $10 a day. "According to UNICEF, 22,000 children die each day due to poverty. And they 'die quietly in some of the poorest villages on earth, far removed from the scrutiny and the conscience of the world. Being meek and weak in life makes these dying multitudes even more invisible in death'" (http://www.globalissues.org/article/26/poverty-facts-and-stats).

Suffering is not just normal pain and difficulty. Suffering is that which make no sense. I go to the gym three days a week, once a year. It doesn't work. At the gym, I'm in pain, but I'm not suffering. There are reasons why I am not in better physical shape. Suffering is that which should not happen, or happens so disproportionately to some and not to others. There is a family in Wilkes-Barre, Pennsylvania, who suffered severe damage to their house in the Susquehanna River floods of 2011. Less than two years later, their lovely and accomplished daughter had just graduated from medical school. She was the kind of medical student who found time to volunteer for service trips in places like Haiti. Less than three weeks after graduating from medical school, she felt ill on a Monday. She was admitted to the hospital, suffering from a rare disorder, and died surrounded by family and friends on Thursday. Both the flood and the death of such a wonderful young person are bad enough, but for one family to suffer both in less than eighteen months? Why is suffering so disproportionately distributed?

If you have the answer to that question, please let us know. All I know is that to deny God, or say that, "If there's all this suffering, God doesn't exist," doesn't help much. Those who don't believe in God are still faced with all the suffering. What to do? We must look to see how God responds to suffering. We need to be the Body of Christ, fed and strengthened by the Eucharist to reach out to those who suffer.

How does the church respond to suffering? Can the church help us walk with the Lord and be on fire with the faith, hope, and love of the Holy Spirit in a world where too many children cry themselves to sleep because their stomachs are empty? How can, how does, the community called church respond to all the suffering and pain of our world?

As a young Jesuit, I learned one lesson about how the church responds to all this from a group of school children at a Catholic school near the Jesuit novitiate in Wernersville, Pennsylvania. I was sent two afternoons a week to teach catechism to fifth and sixth graders. We had a good time. The kids behaved and listened to me, and recess was a time I could show off my athletic skills against boys much younger than I. In class on the first day, I immediately noticed one little girl who was, how can I say this gently, one of the most physically unattractive little girls I had ever seen. She would walk right up to you and say, "I'm ugly. I know I'm ugly. You don't have to pretend you don't notice." My heart ached for this kid, short and pudgy bordering on fat, with stringy hair, a porcine nose and weirdly lopsided eyes. What surprised me after getting to know the class was how well all the other kids treated this little girl. She wasn't picked on. The other kids just treated her like one of the gang. After a few weeks, I commented on this phenomenon to the sixth-grade teacher. She replied, "Watch Tracey." Tracey was this tall, beautiful, blue-eyed blond. She was articulate and smart with a sparkling personality. Even more, she was a natural leader. All the kids in the class took their cues from Tracey. She was an alpha girl, a queen bee, who used her power to help, not oppress, others. Although Tracey could have been a "mean girl," the real mean girls never want to mix it up with the Traceys of the world. As I observed the social interaction of the kids more closely, I noticed it was communicated to the class, in ways subtle and beautiful, that the unattractive little girl was Tracey's friend. Anyone who messed with the little girl would answer to Tracey, and no one wanted to mess with Tracey.

I trust it was something in the Catholic atmosphere of that school that enabled and encouraged Tracey to be the way she was. The Philly IHM sisters who ran the school were constantly preaching that concern for others is a hallmark of Catholic schools. Tracey and that class got the message.

How do we think about and respond to suffering? Are we hopeful or despondent in the face of life's pain and suffering? There's an old story about a father who has two little boys, one an incurable optimist and the other a dedicated pessimist. So he decides to try to get his kids to see things with a bit more balance. He goes out and buys a truckload of toys and puts them around the little pessimist's bed. The sun comes through the window in the morning, the kid wakes up, rubs his eyes, and sees all the new toys around his bed and sighs, "What am I going to do with all these toys? I'm going to have to get batteries for them. I'll have to put them away after playing with them. Other kids and my brother will want to play with them. . . ." The father can't believe what he's hearing, so he decides to work on the little optimist. He goes out, gets a truckload of horse manure, and puts it all around the little boy's bed. Sun comes in the window, the kid wakes up and rubs his eyes. He smells and sees the horse manure and leaps up on the bed. He's screaming and yelling for joy. He jumps down in it, throws it in the air, gets it in his hair. At this point his Dad comes in and says, "Wait. Tell me. I don't get it. What could possibly be good about a whole truckload of horse manure?" The kid says excitedly, "Daddy. If there's all this s*#t, I figure there must be a pony!"

It was hard to find the pony on the East Coast of the United States in 2012. It's been even harder at other times. The Tsunami in Sri Lanka and Sumatra on December 26, 2004. Over 200,000 died. That earthquake equaled the energy of 23,000 atomic bombs. Where was God? The Haiti earthquake of 2010: Somewhere between 250,000 and 316,000 people died. Where was God?

Hurricane Sandy, October 29-30, 2012, was a natural disaster that resulted in more than one hundred deaths. A few days later, a freak early snowstorm dumped twelve inches on some of the hardest hit areas. The loss of property and damages was in the tens of billions of dollars.

Newtown, Connecticut, December 14, 2012. Sandy Hook elementary school. An insane twenty-year-old gunman viciously murders twenty first graders and six adults. Other shootings through the years are all too familiar: Columbine, Virginia Tech, and Aurora, Colorado. And the thousands killed in Afghanistan and Iraq since September 11, 2001. And throughout history: estimates of 100,000 dead in Lisbon's 1755 earthquake. The bubonic plague killing one third of Europe's population in the fourteenth century.

Where was God, where is God, in all of this? We know that God is not some "thing" among other things. God is not some old man with a long white beard up in the clouds. God is the love that pulsates as the source and sustainer of all realities. God is in and with all those who respond to those in need.

The truth is that we have to let go of an inadequate image of God. This is the Magic God, the God of the Lottery Ticket. "O God Let *ME* win the millions. . . ." This is the God of "Oh Jesus, I've been drinking and I need to drive home. Don't let the cops stop me and give me a breathalyzer." If you know where this Magic God is, please let me know, because I've never been able to find that God.

There are only two things of which I am absolutely certain: (1) God loves us, and (2) humans suffer. No one has ever disagreed with the second assertion. Because of the experience and reality of suffering, many have questioned the first. And suffering really has no answer. If it made sense, it wouldn't be suffering.

Many say, "I can't believe in a God, or I refuse to accept a God, who would allow such suffering." This is the famous position of Dostoyevsky's Ivan Karamazov, who "returns his entrance ticket." The problem with this way of seeing suffering is that there's still all the pain and suffering. Whether we believe in God or not, there is still suffering. To say there is no God doesn't help us understand anything and doesn't "solve" the problem of suffering.

Really, suffering is only a problem for those who do believe in a loving God, a God who cares about us. If there is no God, if God doesn't exist or love us, then life and its suffering are simply "the way things are," and there is no reason why we should expect that life should be different.

But for those of us who believe, we are challenged by suffering. We have to embrace the God who suffers with us, responds to, and thus transforms, all suffering. We don't have a magic God. We don't have a God who promises us a life without suffering. We don't have a God who says horse manure will smell like roses, or that rainwater will be beer.

We do have a God who promises to ultimately make suffering if not intelligible, at least responded to. "He will wipe every tear from their eyes. There will be no more death or mourning or crying or pain, for the old order of things has passed away" (Rev 21:4). We have a world like the world described by St. Paul in his letter to the Romans: "For the creation waits . . . in hope that the creation itself will be set free from its bondage to decay and will obtain the glory of the children of God" (Rom 8:19-23).

The way Christians see things, creation has gotten off track, way off track, off track in ways we little comprehend, for reasons we cannot fully understand. The world in which we live, human existence itself, is not the way things ought to be. No matter how good our life may be, we, and all creation, suffer. So what does God do? God responds. God comes and saves us. Our faith recognizes the fact of suffering, the reality of suffering, and then looks with the eyes of faith to see how God responds.

This God who responds to human suffering is a fascinating God. This true and living God, this God who responds, is the God of Moses who led the Israelites out of slavery in Egypt. This God becomes "flesh and dwells among us" (John 1:14). This God is "the way, the truth, and the life" (John 14:6), "the Good Shepherd" (John 10), "the Bread of Life" (John 6). This God is the God who says, "Blessed are the poor, the meek, and those who hunger and thirst for justice. Blessed are those who mourn" (Matthew 5). This responding God is the one who raised Lazarus from the dead. This responding God suffered and died on the cross. This responding God is one who enters so deeply into the suffering and pain of human existence that he transforms it, bringing us salvation in and through the resurrection.

This is a suffering God. We all grope toward a God who saves, a God who brings us through the suffering and pain to life and love and holiness and wholeness.

This suffering and responding God was with those two little kids swept out of their mother's arms into the surging waters on Staten Island. This suffering and responding God is with every family that lost house and home and precious possessions: the wedding pictures, the high school yearbook, their favorite Jets jersey. This suffering and responding God died a little with every single one of the hundreds who died that week. And this suffering and responding God rises with everyone who enters eternal life.

This God of the resurrection lives in the heart of everyone who suffers with those who suffer. This God lives in the heart and is revealed in the actions of every person who responds to the suffering and tragedies of human existence.

There is no resurrection without the cross of Christ, which means there is no cross, that is, no suffering, in our lives that does not contain within it the seeds of resurrection. Let us pray at our Masses, at our eucharistic tables, that the God who feeds us will inspire us to feed and clothe and help others. Let us pray that this God with us in the Eucharist will be with those who are suffering, and with those who are helping them. Let us pray this day that God will inspire us to respond, generously, effectively, lovingly to those who suffer tragedy and disasters of all kinds.

Where was God in all of this? Where is God in all of this? God is in the suffering and God is in the response, in our response.

God is in our response when we lovingly and effectively do the work that produces a world of justice and peace. We may not be able to eliminate all pain and suffering, but we can do a much better job of ameliorating conditions for our brothers and sisters than we are doing. Almost 50 percent of those who live on this planet, more than three billion people, exist on less than $2.50 a day. The GDP of 567 million people in desperately poor countries is less than the combined wealth of the world's seven richest people. Nearly a billion people in the twenty-first century cannot read a book or write their names. If we had taken 1 percent of what we spend on weapons in this world, we could send every kid on the globe to school. One billion children suffer in poverty; 640 million don't have decent housing; 270 million have no access to health care. Some 29,000 little kids under the age of five die every day (http://www.globalissues.org/issue/2/causes-of-poverty).

Justice is the work of righting relationships. In 1995, my own religious congregation, the Society of Jesus, tells those of us who are Jesuits, "We are servants of Christ's mission . . . (15). Ours is a service of faith and of the radical implications of faith in a world where it becomes easier to settle for something less than faith and less than justice (36). . . . The promotion of justice requires, before all else, our own continuing conversion (66)" (34th General Congregation, 1995).

In 2008, along with Pope Benedict, we further explicated our mission in relation to justice. "The service of faith and the promotion of justice must be kept united. Pope Benedict reminded us that the injustice that breeds poverty has 'structural causes' which must be opposed. . . . The preferential option for the poor is implicit in the Christological faith in God who became poor for us . . . (6)" (35th General Congregation, 2008).

Social structures affect and contour our choices in multiple and multifaceted manners. A social structure is society's blueprint, the way things are set up, the social positions that maintain a society and determine the opportunities people can hope to have.

I played football for years and scored only one touchdown. The structure of the game means that centers and linebackers almost never carry the ball into the end zone. Birthday parties and weddings are social structures. You can't have a birthday pizza; it has to be a cake. At the start of the wedding, it is still customary for the father to give away the bride, even though the original meaning of the symbol has drastically changed. The woman is no longer given as property to her new husband (we hope!). But the groom's surname is still usually taken by the bride. A classroom is a social structure, and not only the teacher–student relationship but the very fact that where one lives in the United States so determines the quality of education is a social structure crying for remediation. College tuition is set up as an equal charge, even though students and families have vastly different economic resources. Despite the fact that many students receive up to a 40-percent tuition discount on average, it still is surprising that our society says a family that has an annual income of $50,000 is charged as much as the family that has $5 million a year. Even more startling to the students in my classes who are going into deep and dangerous debt to pay for college is the news that, in many countries, college is free. In countries like Greece, Czechoslovakia, Argentina, Ireland, Cuba, and Libya you can go to college without paying. In Iraq, before George W. Bush, education was free through the Ph.D. level. In many Nordic countries, college is free, even for foreign students! The tax code is a social structure, and Warren Buffet has famously questioned the wisdom and sanity of his having to pay only 15 percent of his income in taxes, while his secretary has to pay above 30 percent.

Wages are one of the most complex and confusing social structures. Catholic social teaching has long held that a living wage is a wage that can support a family. In the United States, the minimum wage is $7.25 an hour. That's $14,500 annually, if you can get two thousand hours in a year. Middle-class wages have stagnated since 1973. A Guaranteed Annual Income was an idea championed by well-known economists like Milton Friedman, Friedrich Hayek (http://en.wikipedia.org/wiki/Guaranteed_minimum_income), and politicians Daniel P. Moynihan and Richard Nixon (http://www.nytimes.com/books/98/10/04/specials/moynihan-income.html). Despite ideas floated about structuring wages more equitably, sanely, and justly, efforts to actually do so have gone from sporadic to nonexistent. Still, the fact remains: the $2.75 an hour I earned at minimum wage jobs in the early 1970s would be worth somewhere between $11.50 and $25.30 today (http://www.measuringworth.com/uscompare/relativevalue.php). Yet in 2013, the minimum wage is $7.25 an hour. States that have raised the minimum wage (e.g., New York, Washington, California) have not experienced the negative consequences predicted by conservative pundits.

There have been gains made by a global economy. Poverty "has declined more in the past 50 years than the previous 500. Over the last 50 years, in fact, even while the Earth's population has doubled, the average per capita income globally (adjusted for inflation) has more than tripled" (Diamandis 2012). Still, forty years after LBJ declared war on it, poverty is still rampant in the United States. In 2012, the Associated Press's Hope Yen reported that poverty in the United States has risen to levels not seen since the 1960s (Yen 2012). And poverty rates across the globe are even more extreme.

This idea that we must do justice is not simply the opinion of this "liberal" Jesuit. It is the teaching of our church. "The duty of making oneself a neighbor to others and actively serving them becomes even more urgent when it involves the disadvantaged, in whatever area this may be. 'As you did it to one of the least of these my brethren, you did it to me'" (Matt 25:40, quoted in CCC §1932). The "sinful inequalities" affecting billions on our planet "are in open contradiction of the Gospel" (CCC §1938).

What does the church call us to do? We must practice solidarity. This is a "direct demand" of us as Christians (CCC §1939). "Solidarity is manifested in the first place by distribution of goods and remuneration for work. It also presupposes the effort for a more just social order where tensions are better able to be reduced and conflicts more readily settled by negotiation" (CCC §1940). The *Catechism* goes on to argue that socioeconomic inequalities can be addressed and "resolved only with the help of all the forms of solidarity: solidarity of the poor among themselves, between rich and poor, of workers among themselves, between employers and employees in business, solidarity among nations and peoples. International solidarity is a requirement of the moral order; world peace in part depends upon this" (CCC §1941). Most tellingly and challengingly, "The equal dignity of human persons requires the effort to reduce excessive social and economic inequalities" (CCC §1947). The U.S. Catholic bishops proclaim:

> As followers of Christ, we are challenged to make a fundamental "option for the poor"—to speak for the voiceless, to defend the defenseless, to assess life styles, policies and social institutions in terms of their impact on the poor. This option for the poor does not mean pitting one group against another, but rather strengthening the whole community by assisting those who are most vulnerable. As Christians, we are called to respond to the needs of all our brothers and sisters, but those with the greatest needs require the greatest response. (USCCB 1986, §16)

This is not some new view that came in with liberation theology or the social encyclicals of John Paul II. This has been the stance of the church ever since Jesus said, "Blessed are the poor" (Matthew 5). In the fourth century, St. Ambrose taught, "You are not making a gift of your possessions to the poor person. You are handing over to him what is his. For what you have been given in common for the use of all, you have arrogated to yourself. The world is given to all, and not only to the rich." And to the retort, "Well Father, Jesus did say the poor we would always have with us," I reply, "Take a closer look. Jesus said that to Judas" (John 12:4-8).

The justice of Jesus is rooted in love. Justice, the work of righting relationships, starts with the first step of respecting and loving ourselves. Much of the inhumanity and pain we inflict on one another and the inability to confront our sinfulness and the sinfulness of the social structures of our world are rooted in our own deeply distorted sense of ourselves as unlovable and therefore unable to love. The fascinating founder of L'Arche, Jean Vanier, writes:

> The first choice, at the root of all human growth, is the choice to accept ourselves; to accept ourselves as we are, with our gifts and abilities, but also our shortcomings, inner wounds, darkness, faults, mortality; to accept our past and family and environment, but equally our capacity for growth; to accept the universe with its laws, and our place at the heart of the universe. Growth begins when we give up dreaming about ourselves and accept our humanity as it is, limited, poor but also beautiful. Sometimes the refusal to accept ourselves hides real gifts and abilities. The dangerous thing for human beings is to want to be other than they are, to want to be someone else, or even want to be God. We need to be ourselves, with our gifts and abilities, our capacity for communion and co-operation. This is the way to be happy. (Vanier 2008, 122)

Official church teaching states, "Social Justice can be obtained only in respecting the transcendent dignity of man. The person represents the ultimate end of society, which is ordered to him" (CCC §1929).

Can the world become a better place? A few years ago, I was teaching an Introduction to Sociology course, and I'd labored mightily to inspire in my students an awareness of the basic principles of Catholic Social Teaching and how the implementation of such principles could make the world so much better. I noticed Charley in the back looking bored out of his mind. He was usually with the program, so I called to him, "Yo, Charley! What's up? You look amazingly uninterested in all this." He replied, "No offense Padre, but this is all just so much BS. Everything is all screwed up and nothing is ever going to get any better. Nothing will ever change." This was well before 2008 when much opportunity really did go down the drain economically for young adults in the United States. But that day I realized that one of my main duties as a teacher is to try to help young adults see that our world is wonderful and can become a real paradise in the twenty-first century, if we handle the problems facing us as a human family. Too many of my students seem to accept without question the assessment that "things are getting worse." I challenge them to think critically (Is "x" true? Is "x" right and just? Is "x" good?). I argue that we live in amazing and wonderful times. Just think. One hundred years ago we had so little of what we take for granted today, things millions on this planet have only seen on television. Electricity. Computers. Cheap books. Hot showers. Flush toilets. More food than we can eat. Yes, there are wars and rumors of wars and wars that cost exorbitantly ($3 trillion on Afghanistan and Iraq). But think back just seventy years ago. Most of the planet was trying to blow each other off the face of the earth. Fifty million people died in World War II—50 percent of them civilian—and millions more in World War I. In 1919, millions died from the flu.

I tell students that I was born three months before Rosa Parks refused to give up her seat. There's no connection between the two events except in my own mind. But I was born into a United States of America were segregation was legal, lethal, and largely unquestioned. If you did question the status quo, they wouldn't just yell about you on "shock and yell" radio and TV cable shows. They would kill you. There are over forty martyrs commemorated at the Civil Rights Museum in Montgomery, Alabama. Many of them were young people no older than the college students seated before me. Andrew Goodman was twenty years of age when he was murdered near Philadelphia, Mississippi, in 1964, along with James Chaney, 21, and Mickey Schwerner, 24. The local Ku Klux Klan along with civil authorities, including the Nashoba county deputy sheriff, conspired to kill them.

By July of 1964, when I'm eight years old, Lyndon Baines Johnson, a southern senator from Texas and then president, signs the Civil Rights Act, one of the great moments in American history. And to show how far we have come, look at a picture of the signing. There are dozens of people behind President Johnson. And not one of them is a woman. No signing of such magnitude would occur today in Washington without women being present.

Today, if you have solutions to our problems, no one will kill you. If you can figure out how to deal with global weather change, prison reform, and the amelioration of the criminal justice system, gender equality, eradicating human trafficking, immigration reform, global peace and an end to war, clean and renewable energy, the list goes on and on, they will give you the Nobel Prize.

Things not only are getting better. Things can be amazingly repaired and reconciled. In her amazing memoir of the Rwandan genocide of April-July 1994, Immaculée Ilibagiza shares how she survived the horrors of the killing, hidden in a cramped bathroom with seven other women for three months (http://www.lefttotell.com/). Immaculée was twenty-two years old when the insane frenzied outbreak of brutal and violent tribal animosity killed most of her family. The majority Hutus murdered some one million of the minority Tutsis in less than four months, some 20 percent of the population of the country. Twenty percent of the United States would be sixty-three million people, roughly the population of the states of Pennsylvania, New York, New Jersey, Maryland, Connecticut, Massachusetts, and Virginia.

The most remarkable reality of her story is how prayer sustained her through the long days and longer nights as she huddled in that overcrowded bathroom, while she heard the cries and tears of those being butchered outside the window. Even more remarkable is the way prayer brought her to forgive those who perpetrated the genocide (Ilibagiza 2007). Her testimony is one of the most amazing witnesses to the power of prayer to work reconciliation and forgiveness in the history of Christianity.

On September 11, 1973, Chile suffered a coup d'état of President Salvador Allende's government, orchestrated by the Chilean military, assisted and fomented by operatives of the U.S. government. Some three thousand Chileans were murdered in the aftermath, as General Pinochet's military government and secret police (DINA [Dirección de Inteligencia Nacional]) mercilessly persecuted those deemed "Marxist." In the days after the coup, suspects were herded into the Estadio Chile, the National Stadium of Chile. Among the estimated thirty thousand to fifty thousand detained, many were executed. Victor Jara, Chile's most famous folk singer, whose Nueva Canción Chilena movement had elicited hope of justice and peace among Chile's and all of Latin America's impoverished masses, was taken to the stadium on September 12, 1973. He was mercilessly beaten. Some reports say his hands were broken. One account I heard in Chile in the early 1980s was that his hands were cut off and the persecutors handed him a guitar and said, "Go ahead. Play now *Huevon*" (untranslateable—something like our "A**hole"). Those imprisoned and tortured with Jara testified that he defiantly sang the anthem "*Venceremos*" ("We will win"). After four days in captivity, Jara was shot to death by machine gun; forty-four bullets were found in his body after it was dumped in a Santiago shantytown. Years later, after the decades-long struggle to oust General Pinochet, and the slow reestablishment of democratic and sane government in Chile, the National Stadium, the sight of so much torture and terror in the 1970s, was renamed Estadio Victor Jara. The avenue named "11 de Septiembre" proudly commemorating the coup has been renamed "Avenida Nueva Providencia," New Providence Avenue (Rooney 2013).

Another Chilean woman knew of her father, an Air Force general, being tortured daily for months by Pinochet's minions. As a result of the constant torture sessions, the general died of a heart attack while in prison. The young woman and her mother were also taken and tortured for twenty-one days in the hell of the Villa Grimaldi detention center. Once released, they had to go into exile to protect and save their lives. That young woman returned years later and became the president of Chile. I don't know if President Bachelet has forgiven those who tortured her, but she certainly is not consumed and controlled by hatred and anger for those who so grievously wronged her and her family. Michelle Bachelet demonstrates that Chileans have moved beyond the nightmare of the Pinochet years.

When I was in Chile in the early 1980s, a woman was taken and raped and tortured by Pinochet's secret police. They wanted to know where her son was. She did not know. After her horrific ordeal, she was freed through the intervention of the Archdiocese of Santiago's *Vicariate de la Solidaridad*. At a press conference organized to publicize and denounce the incident, the woman was asked what she wanted done to those who tortured her. I'll never forget her reply. "*O, soy Catolica. Les perdono. Hay que ser enfermos mentales*" ("Oh, I am a Catholic. I forgive them. They must be mentally ill").

Immaculée Ilibagiza, Victor Jara, Michelle Bachelet, the Chilean woman who forgave her torturers—they all exemplify the greatest challenge of Jesus' way of being: We need to forgive one another. True justice, transformative justice, is rooted in reconciliation.

On February 3, 1998, the State of Texas executed Karla Fay Tucker, a young woman who had murdered Ron Carlson's sister, Deborah. Karla Fay was high on drugs at the time as she hacked Deborah to death with a pick-axe. For months, Ron was filled with anger and rage, succumbing to the self-medication of alcohol and drugs, mired in a state of heart that could only be healed by a profound experience of the Holy Spirit. Ron states:

> Then one night, I just couldn't take it anymore. I guess I had come to the point where I knew I had to do something about the hatred and rage that was building in me. It was getting so bad that all I wanted to do was destroy things and kill people. I was heading down the same path as the people who had killed my sister and my dad. Anyway, I opened a Bible, and began to read. It was really weird. I was high—I was smoking doobies and reading the word of God! But when I got to where they crucified Jesus, I slammed the book shut. For some reason it struck me like it never had before: My God, they even killed Jesus! Then I got down on my knees—I'd never done this before—and asked God to come into my life and make me into the type of person he wanted me to be, and to be the Lord of my life. That's basically what happened that night. Later I read more, and a line from the Lord's Prayer—this line that says "forgive us as we forgive"—jumped out at me. The meaning seemed clear: "You won't be forgiven until you forgive." I remember

arguing to myself, "I can't do that, I could never do that," and God seemed to answer right back, "Well, Ron, *you* can't. But through me you can." (Arnold 2010, 88-89)

Ron Carlson eventually visited and got to know Karla Fay Tucker. She too had had a profound experience of the Lord while in prison. Ron came to forgive her and was present at her execution, seated with Tucker's friends and family, not with the families of the victims of her crime.

In 1995, the Society of Jesus, the Jesuits, promulgated a document defining who and what we hope to be. In "Servants of Christ Mission," we stated, "Jesuits in North America are dealing with the challenges of new forms of cultural and economic deprivation. They work in close cooperation with many others in trying to influence the complex structures of society where decisions are made and values are shaped" (34th General Congregation, §22). Our societies across the globe need to be formed and fashioned, that is, structured, in ways that make it more likely that we will want to be just, merciful, and loving. Our schools and other apostolates must call our political and economic institutions to inculcate and embody the peace and justice for all that we all deeply desire. This is not easy.

> We recognize, along with many others, that without faith, without the eye of love, the human world seems too evil for God to be good, for a good God to exist. But faith recognizes that God is acting through Christ's love and the power of the Holy Spirit, to destroy the structures of sin which afflict the bodies and hearts of his children. Our Jesuit mission touches something fundamental in the human heart: the desire to find God in a world scarred by sin, and then to live the Gospel in all its implications. (34th General Congregation, §36)

Jesuits noted,

> This faith in God is inescapably social in its implications, because it is directed towards how people relate to one another and how society should be ordered. . . . When a society has no moral and spiritual basis, the result is conflicting ideologies

of hatreds which provoke nationalistic, racial, economic and sexual violence. This in turn multiplies the abuses that breed resentments and conflict. . . . Society then falls prey to the powerful and manipulative. (34th General Congregation, §37).

Despite the ever-present struggles for power, possessions, and pleasure, there is hope. "But a faith that looks to the Kingdom generates communities which counter social conflict and disintegration. From faith comes the justice willed by God. . . . religious faith, as the inspiration of the human and social good found in God's Kingdom, that alone can take the human family beyond decline and destructive conflict" (34th General Congregation, §37). Justice is what love looks like in action. "Justice can truly flourish only when it involves the transformation of cultures, since the roots of injustice are imbedded in cultural attitudes as well as in economic structures" (34th General Congregation, §42). Pope Francis said it best in a World Youth Day address entitled "The Humblest Offer the World a Lesson in Solidarity."

> I would like to make an appeal to those in possession of greater resources, to public authorities and to all people of good will who are working for social justice: never tire of working for a more just world, marked by greater solidarity! No one can remain insensitive to the inequalities that persist in the world! Everybody, according to his or her particular opportunities and responsibilities, should be able to make a personal contribution to putting an end to so many social injustices. The culture of selfishness and individualism that often prevails in our society is not what builds up and leads to a more habitable world: it is the culture of solidarity that does so, seeing others not as rivals or statistics, but brothers and sisters. (Pope Francis 2013)

CHAPTER 7

Sacraments Sing Our Stories

A sacrament is that which achieves in human hearts and minds, what it signifies to human minds.

—Brian Daley, S.J.

A sacrament is physical, and within it is God's love; as a sandwich is physical, and nutritious and pleasurable, and within it is love, if someone makes it for you and gives it to you with love . . . then God's love too is in the sandwich.

—Dubus, "Sacraments," 220

It's good to do uncomfortable things. It's weight training for life.

—Lamott, *Plan B,* 200-201

The great short story writer Andre Dubus tells of making sandwiches for his children as he manipulates the challenges of doing so in a kitchen designed for his wheelchair. Sacraments are the living embodiment of how God loves us and the source of power and grace impelling us to do the often hard work of loving one another. Dubus writes, "I need sacraments I can receive through my senses. I need God manifested as Christ, who ate and drank and shat and suffered and laughed. So I can dance with Him as the leaf dances in the breeze under the sun" (Dubus 2000, 221-22).

There's the story of little three-year-old Barney who was upset after his little sister's baptism. His dad asked what was bothering him.

"That priest. He says we're going to live in a good Christian home."
"Yeah, so what's the matter with that?" Barney cries, "I want to stay with you guys." Sacraments aren't magic. Sacraments work by giving us grace and giving us the power and strength we need to be followers of Jesus and his agents in establishing the reign of God in our personal and social lives. Sacraments help us be good Christians.

When I was seven, Miss Stanton, our second-grade teacher (a nineteen-year-old young woman working her way through college by teaching us), prepared the sixty-five of us second graders for our first confessions. Sr. Grace Marian, RSM, who had the horde of us the year before, helped out. On hearing that we could be forgiven for anything and everything, I was stunned. This was the best deal I'd ever heard of. Soon I was hard at work on my list. Disobeying my parents three million times. Fighting with my brother five million times. Lying about washing my hands before dinner, or brushing my teeth before bed, one million times. I usually did those two things, but I thought this was a chance to get everything wiped out. New start. New day. I kept working on my list and didn't show it to anybody, because all this was under something called the seal of confession, whatever that meant. All I knew was that I could say all this stuff to the priest, he couldn't tell anybody, and I'd be off the hook. For good and forever. Cool. Very cool.

We'd be in the confessional box; we'd been taken over a week before to get used to the darkness and sliding screen between the priest and the person confessing. A few days before the Friday morning when we were going to be taken over to the church for our first confessions, Sr. Grace Marian sat up front like the priest and had some kids kneel next to the screen to her left and go through the routine so we'd all get it down. "Bless me Father for I have sinned. This is my First Confession. These are my sins." Then my buddy Frankie gets up there and he's saying he'd lied three times, he'd fought with his brother Pat two times ... heck, I'd fought with both him and Pat more times than that. Than Marcia went up, and she's such a teacher's pet, but she's saying she disobeyed her parent twice and lied once but then told her mother she'd lied, so it hardly even counted. I'm getting nervous. Is everyone really only going with single digits? Come on. We all know the numbers are a lot higher. My lowest number is a million.

The big day arrives, and I'm still in a quandary. No one said much about number of times. Am I the only one who is going to be honest? Or am I the only one who is so bad? I mean I know I flunked self-control three marking periods. But what will the priest say when he hears my millions? I'll be saying penance prayers for months. How about I just go with smaller numbers? Maybe a dozen this and two dozen that. But I know I've fought with my brother at least several million times.

Still, this is a deal. I can say it all and the priest can't tell anybody. I can get a new start. So with my little heart pounding I push through the mega heavy velvet curtain of the confessional box. It's a hot day in May and the church is sweltering. I'm in the middle of the pack (everything in Catholic school was done in alphabetical order). I'm happy because Mike Fitz had whispered to me that he'd gotten Fr. Delaney. I was in line for the same box and liked Fr. Delaney. He was really old and was friendly to us little kids. So were all the priests, but I figured Fr. Delaney would be especially lenient.

The outer plastic slider slid and there is Fr. Delaney behind the second screen. I screw up all the courage a seven-year-old can muster and go for it. "Bless me Father for I have sinned, this is my First Confession . . ." and I immediately launch into my list of several million this and this many millions that. After I've breathlessly gotten through my rather long list of huge numbers of sins, there is a stunned silence on Fr. Delaney's side of the slide. Is he mad? Am I the worst he's ever heard? Am I in trouble? Will he have to tell Sr. Teresa, the principal, and I'll have to sit in her office again? But he's not mad. I realize he's laughing and trying to stifle it, but can't. Soon he's laughing so hard and so loud, I'm sure the whole, quiet church can hear. "Son," he gasps between breaking into more laughs, "that's the best I've heard all day. Three Hail Marys and three Our Fathers. Go in peace." Yes! This is great.

I walk out and Miss Stanton and Sr. Grace Marian are standing in the aisle down from the confessional box. They look at me with wide eyes and open mouths, with that look that lets me know I've amazed and mystified them once again. Feeling wonderful, I head up to the altar rail to kneel and say my penance. Everything I've ever done wrong is gone. I can start all over. Best "do over" in the world. Years later, after having had the privilege of hearing First Confessions myself, I realize what a memorable moment I must have given Fr. Delaney.

St. Thomas Aquinas realized that grace is operating when we find ourselves able to do what we could not do before (Connor 2006, 263). My old theology professor Jesuit Father Brian Daley, S.J., taught us "a sacrament is that which achieves in human hearts and minds, what it signifies to human minds." Famous Jesuit theologian Karl Rahner cogently presents a fascinating schema for how sacraments work. His seminal article "The Theology of the Real Symbol" argues that any reality becomes what it is in its relationship with an "other." We need to be in relationship to become real as the children's stories *The Velveteen Rabbit* and *The Giving Tree* so charmingly reveal to minds young and old.

Rahner teaches that anything becomes its real self by giving itself as gift to the other. We become our true and real selves in others. Parents become themselves in their children; doctors and nurses become their real selves in their patients; teachers become their real selves in their students. Rahner demonstrates that God becomes God's real self in Jesus and Jesus becomes Jesus' real self in the church, while the church becomes the church's real self in the sacraments. This sacramental causality is experienced when we feel the freedom and appropriate the authenticity of allowing the Holy Spirit to set us on fire as a result of entering into the sacraments (Rahner 1966, 234, 239-41).

Notre Dame theologian Richard McBrien teaches that "the principle of sacramentality [is] the fundamentally Catholic notion that all reality is potentially and in fact the bearer of God's presence and the instrument of divine action on our behalf" (McBrien 1981, 1225). This is central to Catholic ways of being and perceiving the meanings of our lives. We experience that things are more than just things. The realities of our lives, the tangible physical things and the more immaterial parts (e.g., memory, will, hopes, fears, and dreams) of our human existence are charged through with the pulsating power and presence of God. Things carry meanings. Some things are just for fun, for example, a red baseball cap with a "P" means something to a Philadelphia kid. Some things are functional: radio waves were always there; it took Maxwell, Hertz, and Marconi to come along and harness the power and possibilities of those realities. Both sports and science speak of the fun and wonder of the world. And some things reveal transcendence to us. Bread and wine blessed and consecrated are much more than wheat and grape. They are the reality of God with us. Sacraments focus our attention on key realities, relational realities, of our lives, which reveal in ways wondrous and transformative the grace and love of God.

There's an old joke about the guy who is walking down the street and he hears a voice say, "Stop!" He stops and a huge rock falls onto the sidewalk right where he would have been walking. He asks, "Who are you?" and the voice answers, "I'm your guardian angel." He gets in his car and drives a few blocks and is approaching an intersection and the voice yells, "Stop!" He jams on the brakes and screeches to a halt even though the light is green. He watches in amazement as a huge truck runs the red light. He would have been squashed like a bug. Again he asks, "Who are you?" and hears, "I'm your guardian angel." He gets to his job as a stockbroker and is soon immersed in the world of stress and screens that is money making these days. As he's about to click and buy hundreds of thousands of dollars worth of a stock, he hears the voice say deeply and slowly, "Stop!" He holds off clicking and watches, stunned as the stock price begins dropping. If he had clicked, he would have lost millions for his firm. He says again, "Who are you?" "I'm your guardian angel," says the voice. "So, tell me, where the hell were you when I got married seven years ago?"

Although guardian angels don't tell us next week's lottery numbers, the idea that they exist and affect our lives is both intriguing and comforting. The hope that our saints are close and that we can be in relationship with "those who have gone before us marked with the sign of faith" (Eucharistic Prayer I) is awe inspiring. The idea that there is more to reality than meets the eye runs deep in Catholic sensibilities and styles. Even as normal a reality as disciplining children reveals much about who we are and how we relate to one another and God.

When I was a little kid one thing (among many others) drilled into us was that we were not to throw snowballs at cars. I was in second grade. There's nothing like the excitement among seven-year-olds as snow starts falling outside. After school, we ran out the door and found that the streets had been transformed, blanketed white by a few inches. When Frankie and Pat and I were walking home from school, cars were rolling by us. Soon Pat and Frankie were throwing snowballs. I resisted temptation for about three seconds before joining right in. Frankie was even putting small rocks in the snowballs to give them weight. We were nailing cars from behind parked vehicles where we were hiding, and drivers were hitting the brakes and yelling, shall we say, strong Philly expletives at us (Hey, it's a rough but weirdly loving town). I heard a car approaching, stood up and threw one and nailed the windshield. The car braked and swerved, and I stuck up my little head to see the driver's rage. He was yelling and then I looked at the car behind his. I found myself staring into my father's eyes. He rolled down the window and said, "Ricky, go home. Now."

Now, I knew I was in trouble, and I knew this meant "the belt." Don't jump to conclusions. In the early 1960s, corporal punishment was considered good parenting. My dad never hit us when he was mad. And we never got hit very hard. He had this whole routine. He'd always call you into the kitchen at exactly 8:00 P.M. All afternoon and through dinner, all the other kids would be looking at me and whispering to each other, "Ricky's gonna get it." The waiting was the worst part of it all.

At 8:00 P.M., he'd put down his pipe and paper and said, "Ricky, let's go." He'd always have this long talk, making me explain that I understood what I had done, why it was wrong and why I was getting "the belt." Then he would talk for a long time, saying all the stuff he always said. It would always end with, "this is going to hurt me more than it hurts you." He was right about that. He never hit very hard. Again, it was the whole message of the ritual that mattered. But this time I figured I had a good excuse. I was going to blame my buddies.

"Pat and Frankie were throwing snowballs too. They made me do it. You can't hit me unless you punish them too." Fair was fair. My argument made sense to me.

My father replied, "Their Daddy will take care of disciplining Frankie and Pat. You are my son. You are my responsibility. You are bone of my bone and flesh of my flesh. You are my blood. What you do reflects on me and your mother and all in our family. What you did could have seriously hurt someone. If you hurt someone, I could never forgive myself. I have to teach you how to be a good boy and grow to be a good man. That's my job." Then he said, "This is going to hurt me more than it will hurt you. . . ."

That day I learned I was part of something greater than myself. My family was affected by what I did or did not do.

Family is the first school of faith and also the most powerful instrument in developing a sacramental imagination. We can give our children a sense and felt experience that all of reality is imbued with the mysterious presence of God "deep down things," or we risk allowing their imaginations to atrophy and their hearts to constrict because all of their experiences run no deeper than shallow sit-coms or facile relationships on Facebook. Making kids go to church is hard work, but it's worth it. They will also know how not to make fools of themselves when they go to a grandparent's funeral (e.g., the grand-children of Walt Kowalski [Clint Eastwood] in *Gran Torino*).

Anne Lamott, one of our most spirited and iconoclastic spiritual writers, says it very well.

Why make a kid go to church? I know that Sam believes that Jesus is true. . . . But he hates church. Then why do I make him go? Because I want him to. . . . I want him to see the people who loved me when I felt most unlovable, who have loved me since I first told them I was pregnant. He gets the most valuable things I know through osmosis. Also, he has no job, no car, no income. He needs to stay in my good graces. . . . While he lives at my house, he has to do things my way. And there are worse things for kids than to have to spend time with people who love God. Teenagers who do not go to church are adored by God, but they don't get to meet some people who love God back. Learning to love back is the hardest part of being alive. . . . . Showing up is the lesson. The singing is the lesson, and the power of community. I can't get this to him in a nice package, like a toaster or a pastry or take-out. So every two weeks, I make him come to church with me. (Lamott 2005, 195-96)

Sacraments don't, really can't, have any power or strength or meaning in our lives unless we do them often, repeatedly. You can't watch the final World Series game and have anywhere near the joy true and long Phillies fans had in 1980 and 2008 if you only pay attention to baseball once a year. The World Cup means little to most North Americans. To the rest of the world, it's a sacred time, a month to stop working and watch Fútbol. Children, especially teens, need to be schooled in these matters of sacred times, sacred realities, sacred meanings.

After the song, the teens trudged off together, avoiding eye contact with the rest of us. They're distrustful and spiky—life is weird and doesn't deliver, and adults try to lead them like horses in the direction they think will make them happy, yet for the most part they don't want to go. But the teenagers cannot make the congregation stop smiling at them; they can't make them stop singing, or blessing them. (Lamott 2005, 200)

Sacraments are not easy. Developing a taste for the sacraments is a hard diet for those raised on fast food. Sacraments smack us in the face with the truths that we need God and one another to make it through life. We do not enter eternal life alone.

Of course he doesn't want to come to regular worship—it's so naked, built on the rubble of need and ruin, and our joy is deeply uncool.—But he doesn't want to floss or do homework either. He does not want to have any hard work, ever, but I can't give him that without injuring him. It's good to do uncomfort-able things. It's weight training for life. (Lamott 2005, 200-201)

For many of us, the seven sacraments are complemented by the small sacramentals of life, everything from the Rosary to family meals, to reunions of the clan, to our daily practices that get us in touch with God, "normal" things we do that make us aware of God's goodness and grace in our lives.

One of the most common practices of our culture and times is viewing movies. Much of what Hollywood produces is anything but sacramental, but there are hundreds of wonderful movies that can speak to us of God and help us know God's presence and ways in our lives. From the immigrants' church elbowing its way into American society with Spencer Tracey in *Boys Town* (1938), Bing Crosby in *Going My Way* (1944) and *The Bells of St. Mary's* (1945) to the Oscar-winning *On the Waterfront* (1954), a fictional depiction of a real-life Jesuit priest's efforts to bring justice to the New York Waterfront, to Otto Preminger's homage to the Church Triumphant in *The Cardinal* (1963) to the ever popular *The Sound of Music* (1965) to Kevin Smith's irreverent, but theologically probing *Dogma* (1999) to the painful themes of *Doubt* (2008), Catholicism has been a central pre-occupation for Hollywood. Just look at Martin Scorsese's work. And on the one-hundredth anniversary of movies in 1995, the Vatican released a list of the top forty-five films of all time (http://nccbuscc. org/movies/vaticanfilms.shtml).

Movies are the parables and scriptures of our times. Many college students can quote scores of movie lines but look blankly when they hear supposedly well-known biblical references like the Prodigal Son or the multiplication of the loaves and fishes. Every college student knows *The Godfather* movies; very few have read the entire sixteen chapters of the Gospel of Mark. Too many have seen *Animal House* and *Old School* multiple times; they have never heard of *A Man for All Seasons* or *The Mission*.

Great Movies

It's a Wonderful Life, Places in the Heart, The Shawshank Redemption, The Milagro Beanfield War, While You Were Sleeping, Love Actually, The Mission, Black Robe, Star Wars, Country, Silkwood, On the Waterfront, Mississippi Burning, Blade Runner, Malcolm X, Spartacus, Gallipoli, Schindler's List, Gentleman's Agreement, A Raisin in the Sun, Guess Who's Coming to Dinner, The Color Purple, Driving Miss Daisy, Mississippi Masala, Cry Freedom, Come See the Paradise, Roger and Me, Sicko, Wall Street, Grand Canyon, Six Degrees of Separation, The Fisher King, Awakenings, Breaking Away, Moonstruck, Hoop Dreams, Angels in the Outfield, Rainman, Forrest Gump, Ordinary People, True Lies, Field of Dreams, The Big Chill, Nobody's Fool, Chariots of Fire, Purple Rose of Cairo, The Accidental Tourist, My Bodyguard, Dominick & Eugene, Parenthood, My Left Foot, Lady Sings the Blues, The Little Mermaid, The Lion King, Disney's Hunchback of Notre Dame, Ben-Hur, The Robe, A Man for All Seasons, Dead Man Walking, Cool Hand Luke, Starman, Tender Mercies, Bamboozled, Hurricane, Erin Brockovich, Gladiator, Magnolia, The Matrix, Life Is Beautiful, Gran Torino, Despicable Me, The Lord of the Rings, and many more . . .

When I was a little kid, they used to have these summer programs on the hot, local playground. The bigger girls would teach us how to make lanyards out of gimp, and the teenage boys would run kick ball and dodge ball games. On really hot days, they'd march us into a hot gym, where the ninety-eight degrees outside was ninety-two degrees and show us a movie. During a lot of movies, Frankie and Pat and I would crawl under seats and sneak up on some unsuspecting kid and whap him in the head and generally cause mayhem. But one day they showed *Spencer's Mountain* (1963). I was glued to my seat.

It was the story of a family, their struggles and love for one another, and the sacrifices parents make for children. Clay Spencer (Henry Fonda) is a miner, a hardworking man whose wages barely keep his large family afloat. When his son Clayboy (James McArthur) wants to go to college, Clay has to make a sacrifice. First, Clay sacrifices his pride and asks for a loan from a rich man who spends his money on loose women and other pleasures. The guy has no desire to help the Spencers. So Clay has to make a greater sacrifice. He had been building a wooden "dream house" up on Spencer's Mountain. He and his brothers spent days off on the mountain building a home with a stunning view of magnificent mountains, a mansion in comparison to the cramped, company shotgun house they live in near the mine. I was stunned as Clay set fire to the wooden frame of the dream house. He comes home and asks his wife (Maureen O'Hara) if she would mind living in their tiny house for the rest of their lives. She says not at all. This was the home where her babies were born. "The house on the mountain. That was your dream Clay." "I sold it tonight. Now, Clayboy can go to that there college." Clay Spencer gave up his dream so his boy could have a better life. The movie moved me deeply. I sat there stunned by the magnificent scenery. It was filmed in Wyoming's Grand Teton mountains. I just wanted to go live there. And I wanted a family like the Spencers. The movie was based on the life and novel of Earl Hammer, who went on to write the TV series *The Waltons*.

In recent years, *The Shawshank Redemption* (1994) has grown in popularity after having a middling successful run in theaters. The Internet Movie Database (IMDB) rates it as the number one movie as ranked by its users. The movie is the story of Andy Dufresne (Tim Robbins), a man wrongly convicted of the murder of his wife. A banker before being sent to Shawshank prison, Andy survives by forming community, using his talents to serve others in prison, and, ultimately, by holding on to hope. The instrument of his escape and salvation, a small rock chisel, is hidden in his Bible. In the end, he not only escapes; he works justice and exposes the corrupt administration of the warden and guards. He also mediates hope to his best friend in Shawshank, Red (Morgan Freeman), who finds the courage to dream and hope for life beyond the institutionalization that infects a man's mind and soul behind prison walls.

Sally Fields ("You really like me!") won an Oscar for her role as Edna Spalding in *Places in the Heart* (1984). Widowed when her sheriff husband is killed in a tragic accidental shooting by a black teenager, Edna struggles to survive in Depression-era Waco, Texas. The local community lynches the young man who shot her husband, revenge Edna and her sister neither ask for nor condone. Otherwise, Edna is on her own. The local banker, Mr. Denby (a jibe at director Robert Benton's least favorite movie critic), suggests that she give up her children and sell the small family farm. Instead, she trusts a hobo black man, Moses (Danny Glover), who says he can farm cotton. The banker disapproves, but foists his blind brother-in-law as a boarder on Mrs. Spalding. The development of community among the widow and her children, the blind boarder Mr. Will (John Malkovich) and the sojourner Moses images the biblical community. The final scenes are the best depiction of eschatological reality ever caught on film.

Sandra Bullock's *While You Were Sleeping* (1995) is a gem of a little story teaching a truth I try to impress on college students: you don't marry a person; you marry a family. Lucy is a young woman all alone in the world. It is Christmas Day and she is unhappily working, taking tokens for the Chicago Transit Authority. She sees a man mugged by hoodlums and thrown onto the tracks. Lucy runs out of her booth, jumps down on the tracks, and saves the life of Peter Callaghan. As Peter lies in a coma, through a comic-serious sequence of events, Lucy is mistaken as his fiancée and is quickly adopted and becomes a member of the boisterous, hilarious, very Irish, and very subtly Catholic Callaghan clan. She falls in love with the family, and then Peter's brother, and cannot tell them the truth, for she fears she will lose this great gift of loving relationships that has flooded her life and made her new and whole. The entire movie occurs between Christmas and New Year's Eve. What is really interesting is the way religion quietly plays as an undertone throughout the film.

These movies, and thousands more, are more and more becoming the stories of our lives. We have to learn how to trace the fingerprints of God in the events and stories of our lives, or we will be unable to develop the sacramental imagination needed to live lives rooted in the sacraments. Sacraments, when engaged in regularly and wholeheartedly, transform us and form us into the community called church. Sacraments are "weight training for life." Sacraments give us the strength to go on. To go on believing. To go on loving. To go on mission. Our church has a mission. We are called to change the world. We are to make of our lives a story of mission.

CHAPTER 8

Mission Matters: Jesus says, "Come on, we're going to change the World"

A word from Charles Schulz's Peanuts: Linus is sucking his thumb and holding his blanket to the side of his head saying, "I think the world is much better today than it was five years ago." Charlie Brown waves his arms and yells, "How can you say that? Don't you listen to the radio? Don't you read the papers? How can you stand there and tell me this is a better world?" Linus holds his hand to his heart, drops the blanket by his side and says, "I'm in it now."

Today our prime educational objective must be to form men-and-women-for-others; men and women who will live not for themselves but for God and his Christ—for the God-man who lived and died for all the world; men and women who cannot even conceive of love of God which does not include love for the least of their neighbors; men and women completely convinced that love of God which does not issue in justice for others is a farce.

—Pedro Arrupe, S.J., "Men for Others," speech, Valencia, 1973

The needs of the poor take priority over the desires of the rich; the rights of workers over the maximization of profits; the preservation of the environment over uncontrolled industrial expansion;

the production to meet social needs over production for military purpose.

—USCCB, "Economic Justice for All," §94

Every gun that is made, every warship launched, every rocket fired, signifies in the final sense a theft from those who hunger and are not fed, those who are cold and are not clothed.

—President Dwight D. Eisenhower,
quoted in American Friends Service
Committee, www.oneminuteforpeace.org

One Saturday morning, a guy calls the house of his buddy. The phone is answered and he hears "Hello," whispered by a three-year-old voice. "Hi Billy. Is your daddy there?" "Yes," whispers Billy. "Can I speak with him?" "No," whispers the kid. "Why not?" "He's busy," whispers the little boy. "Well is your mommy there?" "Yes." "Can I speak with her?" "No," whispers Billy. "Why not?" "She's busy," the whispering replies continue. "Look, Billy, I really need to speak to your dad or mom. . . ." Billy breaks in, whispering, "Daddy is talking to the police." "What . . . ?" "Mommy is talking to the firemen." "Billy, the police? The firemen? What's going on over there?" Billy whispers, "Everyone is looking for me."

As Catholics, we are looking for people on fire who want to become men and women on mission, a sending out of companions in the Lord who want to change our world for the better. Like the guy who confronted the bikers five minutes before he arrived in heaven (see intro above), we are called to sacrifice ourselves, our goods, our comfort, and our way of doing things to make a better, more just and more loving world for our brothers and sisters. Here are two examples of the millions who strive to enact the mission, one from real life, one from reel life.

Br. Dennis Jude Ryan, S.J., was born in 1958 and entered the Society of Jesus in 1976, intending to become a Jesuit priest. As a Jesuit novice, he was sent to Red Cloud Indian school at the Jesuit Holy Rosary Mission on the Pine Ridge Reservation in South Dakota and spent most of the next sixteen years (1978-1994) teaching and coaching on the "Res" (reservation). For five of those sixteen years, he spent academic years at Saint Louis University (B.A.) and Boston College (M.A.), studies aimed at increasing his effectiveness to the mission at Pine Ridge.

Pine Ridge is home to the Oglala Sioux, a subgroup of the Lakota nation, the people of Sitting Bull and Crazy Horse. The town of Pine Ridge is about an hour's drive from Wounded Knee. When forced onto the reservation, Chief Red Cloud asked for the "Blackrobes" (before Vatican II in the 1960s, Jesuits wore a distinctive, plain black cassock) despite the fact that Pine Ridge had been assigned to the Episcopalian church in 1875 in order to avoid interdenominational squabbling. The Jesuits established Holy Rosary Mission four miles outside of the town of Pine Ridge in 1888.

Jesuits have been interacting with first peoples since the time of contact between Europeans and the indigenous peoples of the Americas. Jesuit priest Eugene Beuchel, S.J., compiled the first Lakota–English dictionary and grammar. Nick Black Elk of Neihardt's *Black Elk Speaks* (Neihardt 1972) met the Jesuits at Holy Rosary, converted to Catholicism, and spent many years of his life as a Catholic catechist among the people of Pine Ridge (Steltenkamp 1993). The appropriation and acceptance of Christianity by the people of the Oglala, and the transformation of Catholic practice on the Pine Ridge Reservation, are a study in border blending and meaning mixing on both sides.

> Native religion was regarded by the missionaries, particularly the Roman Catholics as the work of the devil. This had an interesting effect on the Oglalas: at the same time that the missionaries were attempting to eradicate all signs of native religion, the Oglalas were positive it worked. Those who subscribed to more than one religion, mainly native religion and Christianity, were regarded as transitional. Even medicine men attended Catholic Mass, participating fully in Holy Communion—according to priests, a sure sign of their Catholicism. (Powers 1977, 114)

The attitudes of the Jesuit priests at Holy Rosary changed as trans-formations in world Catholicism and Catholic theology permeated the globe, especially through the works of Jesuit theologians Karl Rahner and Bernard Lonergan. In the 1950s and 1960s, Jesuit priest Paul Steinmetz redesigned Sacred Heart Church in Pine Ridge, using symbols and images from both the Oglala and Christian traditions. When Steinmetz began to integrate praying with the scared pipe into Catholic rituals, native practitioners of Oglala rituals recognized that one of the Jesuits "had finally seen the light!" (Powers 1977, 116; Steinmetz, 1988). This appreciation for Lakota culture and ways increased through the turbulent years of the 1970s and the resistance at Wounded Knee in 1973.

Some success and much failure, some good and too much evil, have always been present in the missionary efforts of carriers of Euro-pean religious traditions among non-European peoples. The Jesuit order's efforts on Pine Ridge are no exception to the rule. But these efforts, however well-intentioned or misdirected, have been charac-terized as border crossings and boundary blendings, meaning melt-downs and meaning making. What we cannot forget is that there are actual people and lives affected and transformed by these permuta-tions of cultures. The relationships have, at best, always aimed at the establishment of community.

In January 1978, when Dennis Ryan and I arrived at Red Cloud Indian school to engage in the six-month "long experiment" of the Jesuit novitiate (the first two years of the twelve years of prepara-tion for Jesuit priesthood), Red Cloud Indian school (no longer Holy Rosary school) and the Jesuit community were permeated by a conscious attempt to integrate "White" and "Red," Christian and Native religious sentiments and meanings. In 1978, as a young Jesuit, I was introduced to the practice of the sweat lodge by a Jesuit priest, Ron Seminara, S.J., and a local medicine man. The school actively strived to inculcate in the students a sense of pride in their Indian heritage.

Dennis Ryan and I taught in the grade school, drove school buses, coached basketball teams, and did all the tasks that grade school teachers perform. After six months of serving and learning at Red Cloud school, we moved on to philosophy studies in St. Louis.

The experience of the reservation rooted itself deeply in Dennis's soul. His experience of the people of Pine Ridge transformed him. He began to pray and mull over the call to become a Jesuit lay brother, not a priest, in the Society of Jesus. He had been deeply impressed by the lives of quiet and generous self-sacrifice of the Jesuit brothers on the Res, men like Jesuits Br. Bill Siehr and Br. Bill Foster. During Dennis's three years of study at Saint Louis University, he would return again and again to the Res, to work with the Jesuit brothers and to share life with the people of the Oglala. After getting a B.A. at SLU, he went back to Red Cloud to teach, to live, to learn. He was on the Res full time from 1982 to 1985, starting an industrial arts program for the students of Red Cloud. During these years he formalized his commitment to become a Jesuit brother. From 1985 to 1986, he earned a master's degree at Boston College, where he studied the integration of pastoral practice and Oglala culture and folkways. In 1987, he returned to Red Cloud Indian school, where he became the school's assistant principal, the person in charge of discipline. It was said that he was that rare teacher who could tell a kid, "No," and still let the child know that he or she was loved. He was famous for telling corny jokes over the school's public address system. His passion was Red Cloud basketball, and he coached the girls' teams and was assistant coach for the boys' varsity. Coaching in South Dakota meant long, long bus rides to and from games and tournaments. He was a singer with the Red Spirit drum group and was continually taking lessons to improve his speaking of Lakota. He started programs for the students in industrial arts like welding and carpentry.

In order to be closer to the people, Dennis chose to live outside the Red Cloud school–Holy Rosary Mission compound. Dennis lived in a wood burning stove-heated trailer in Oglala, a small village three miles from the school. His pick-up truck was less than a status symbol. Kids from Red Cloud, riding in the beat-up, green pick-up, would duck and hide when they saw friends on the street.

On Saturday, April 16, 1994, at the age of thirty-five, Br. Dennis Ryan, S.J., died suddenly of a massive heart attack. His wake and funeral are a parable, showing what happens when a Jesuit on mission inculturates into the ways and life of the people whom he serves, demonstrating the rich possibilities and powerful conversions made possible and more probable when we strive to form community across cultural and sociopolitical divisions as we live the church's mission.

Some Red Cloud students noticed three eagles circling the South Dakota skies over Red Cloud school the night Dennis died. The northern lights put on a marvelous display that evening. These were taken as signs that Dennis's spirit was rising to the Great Spirit, or Great Mystery, *Wankantanka*. Dennis's life had truly made him included in the Oglala peoples' phrase *Mitak'oyasin* (all my relations). The Saturday evening of his death, and the Sunday morning after, as word spread across the reservation, radio station KILI continually broadcast memorials. Monday morning, the Jesuits gathered the student body and prayed the traditional Catholic liturgical prayers from the Office of the Dead.

Dennis's father and mother, seven brothers and sisters, and over thirty other relatives and friends traveled nine hours by bus from Omaha to Pine Ridge on Tuesday, April 19, 1994. As we crossed onto the reservation, I got on the bus microphone, led the group of pilgrims in prayer, and offered a brief reflection on what this land meant to Dennis, talking about how he and I had started out our Jesuit lives here so many years before, and how Dennis had found his life's purpose and meaning in teaching the children of Red Cloud while living in this starkly beautiful and quiet land. When I sat down, a silence stilled the bus, a quiet that was soon punctured by a voice going on in an evangelical-fundamentalist Christian rhetorical style, a style quite different from that of Omaha's Midwestern Catholicism. It was the bus driver, "witnessing" to us about Christ and the resurrection. We all appreciated his sincerity, but it was the kind of humorous moment Dennis would have loved, me being upstaged by a "Praise the Lord" bus driver!

On arrival at Red Cloud school we were greeted by Jesuits and the people of the school and the Res. We waited for Dennis's body to be brought into Red Cloud school gym for the wake. The gym was decorated with dozens of star quilts, Lakota symbols of life, love, and care, which replaced buffalo robes when buffalo became scarce. Pictures of Dennis, sacred pipes, Catholic rosary beads, sagebrush incense, Bibles, and song sheets in English and Lakota covered tables near where the coffin was placed. The wake lasted into the small hours of the morning. Many local people gave emotional testimonies about Br. Dennis. Throughout the evening, prayers in Catholic and Lakota styles were offered. Prayers with sage incense and the sacred pipe were prayed by medicine men.

In an emotional, candlelit ceremony, the Jesuit superior called roll call for the Red Drum Singers. As each singer's name was called, he indicated his presence by thumping the group's drum. Br. Dennis Ryan's name was called three times and only silence answered. The Red Drum Singers then sang their last song and, to honor Dennis, retired their drum. Br. Dennis's Pow-Wow chair and blanket were presented to Dennis's parents, Leo and Kate Ryan.

The Ryan family and friends were amazed at the outpouring of love and affection expressed for Dennis. The testimonies went on for hours. The review of Dennis's body by the almost one thousand people attending the wake included each person greeting all the members of the Ryan family. The school newspaper captured some of the outpouring of affection for Dennis.

> We do miss you very much, but we have hope we will see you again. If our lights shine like yours, we are promised heaven will be our home. We will all die just like you and take the same journey you took. Denny, just be ready to greet us when it is our turn. Have a joke and a smile waiting for us. I know the Great Spirit has given you a good journey. (Dave & Patricia Brings Plenty and family in *Red Cloud Tribune,* May 6, 1994)

> Denny, these my final words, I won't say "goodbye" to you, But in the tradition of my people, 'Tok'sah Ake' Wacin Yanke Kte' (Someday I will see you again). (A.V. Fire Thunder Class of '95 in *Red Cloud Tribune.* May 6, 1994)

One student wrote Br. Dennis's parents saying, "He was an angel in disguise, helping Lakota children with his love and caring" (Weekly, 1994, p. 3). One of the elders of the Lakota gave Dennis an Indian name, *Lowan hoksila,* meaning "Singing man." To be given such a name by the tribal elders is a great honor. Dennis's parents were presented with an elaborate scroll attesting to Br. Dennis Ryan, S.J., being named an honorary member of the Lakota tribe.

Rapid City bishop Charles Chaput, himself Native American, presided at Br. Dennis's funeral liturgy, which was attended by over one thousand people. The bishop's decorative vestments reflected his native origins, but he did not use the sacred pipe in the funeral liturgy, although sage incense was used. Br. Dennis's coffin was lowered into a wooden box in the hand-dug grave and was nailed shut (after the funeral director jumped in and got the top turned around and placed correctly!). Br. Dennis's body was buried on a small hill above Holy Rosary Mission, next to his hero, Br. Bill Siehr, S.J., and ten yards from the grave of Chief Red Cloud. After his burial, there was a traditional "feed" of stew, *woahjapi,* and fry bread. A traditional "give away" followed the feed, with all of Dennis's family receiving star quilts. The kids from Red Cloud were invited to help themselves to Br. Dennis's large collection of baseball caps.

A year later, the Ryan family and Jesuit community held a traditional giveaway at Red Cloud. The celebration started with a Mass, where Fr. Bill McKinney, S.J., a close friend of Dennis, attributed both Nebraska's football team finally being named Number One, and, more importantly, Red Cloud's basketball team winning the state championship, to Br. Dennis's divine intervention. The congregation proceeded to the graveyard where a star quilt covered Dennis's gravestone. After sage incense was burned and Lakota mourning songs sung, the quilt was removed. On the gravestone is written Br. Dennis J. Ryan, S.J., *Lowan hoksila.* Afterward, a festive atmosphere filled the school dining hall as hundreds received gifts and were filled with the traditional foods of the feed: stew, fry bread, and *woahjapi.*

Br. Dennis Ryan had come to the Res in 1978 as an Irish-Catholic teenager from Omaha. In his short life of three and a half decades, he had crossed borders and bridged boundaries, melding meanings from Omaha to Pine Ridge, from "White" to "Red," from Midwestern, U.S. Catholicism to Lakota religion, from ever rapidly changing North American culture to the enduring culture of the Oglala peoples. In March of 1995, the Red Cloud Crusaders won the South Dakota boys high school basketball championship for the first time ever. The team and coach dedicated the championship to Br. Dennis.

In a short article he wrote for the Minneapolis-Saint Paul Catholic paper, Br. Dennis described his work at Red Cloud Indian school.

> As I grow older, I realize how few answers I really have for people. My time with the Indian people has taught me a great lesson. People appreciate the fact that I show up at community events, whether they be meetings, wakes or pow-wows. Many times here we face senseless and unexplainable death. Young people die from suicide, car wrecks and other accidents. There are no answers for many questions that arise in those situations. But, I find a simple handshake is often enough. People appreciate that I took the time to come. Presence is important. (Ryan 1990).

Br. Dennis's presence and mission on the Res were lived spiritual exercises in the miracle of community, a miracle inherent in many religious traditions. His being was "Lakotaizied" as much as his life and work made the youth of the Oglala more able to survive and thrive both on the Res and in a "White" world beyond the reservation. In his rather short life (by U.S. standards; not by life expectancy on the Res), Br. Dennis's spirit and soul changed, transformed, mixed, and melded with the spirit and soul of the Oglala people. His presence among the people of Pine Ridge also affected them and changed the way they thought about the world and the meaning of life.

The Jesuit presence on the Pine Ridge Reservation can be interpreted in many ways. Some see it as an invasion of a foreign, European body among a Native or First people. But the history of the encounter shows that it is much more complex than that simplistic, politically correct reading. The Jesuits were invited to come to the reservation by Chief Red Cloud. The Jesuits, many of whom have lived the majority of years of their lives on the Res, have adapted their ways, their thinking, even their religious beliefs and practices to be more truly servants of the Lakota peoples to whom they are sent. The life of Br. Dennis and the lives of many other priests and sisters and non-Indians who have had significant contact with the people of the reservation show that cross-cultural contact is a two-way street. The Lakota affect their visitors as much as their visitors affect them. True friends of the Lakota can also serve as liaisons and allies against those who want to continue the exploitation of Native peoples.

Br. Dennis Ryan's life and the lives of those he touched and those who touched him serve as a theological parable and paradigm for awareness of the formation of community's inherent power as we enter into and engage in mission for the third millennium: "We" have much to receive and give with "them" and "they" have much to teach and learn with "us." What happened in Br. Dennis's life can happen to us all in greater or lesser degrees. We all make each other's community and affect one another's lives. Ultimately, we all inhabit a small, blue-brown-white dot, which slowly circles one of four hundred billion stars in the Milky Way galaxy. An awareness of the depth of our kinship and community with one another, and with all peoples, can do much to make human life on this planet more just, more peaceful, and fuller of rich meaning for our earth and all its inhabitants.

From the magic of Hollywood comes another parable of mission, a depiction of what a life of service can intimate for us all. Millions have had their lives and vision transformed through meditating on what for many of us is a yearly ritual, the viewing of Frank Capra's *It's a Wonderful Life*.

> GEORGE BAILEY: *"I've misplaced $8,000. I can't find it anywhere."*
> MR. POTTER: *"You've misplaced it?"*

It's a Wonderful Life isn't just for Christmas. It's a powerful parable to ponder through the year. One person in the story knows what is going on. He knows Potter took the money Uncle Billy absentmindedly leaves in Potter's newspaper. He knows George is frantic and almost suicidal in his need to avoid scandal and prison. He could speak up. But he remains silent. He stands behind Potter's chair and keeps his mouth shut.

Maybe he was afraid for his job. Maybe he really likes the miserly, mean Potter. Maybe he just doesn't want to get involved. But he is involved. He knows. And he does nothing.

George Bailey is the opposite of Potter's servant (slave?). George does get involved. He always does something. He saves his little brother Harry from drowning in the icy, cold pond, losing his hearing in one ear, but indirectly saving hundreds on the troop ship Harry saves years later. George saves Mr. Gower from a prison sentence. George's dreams of traveling the world, building bridges and skyscrapers, disappear in the long years of ten-, twelve-, or fourteen-hour days at the Bailey Building and Loan offices. Rather than let the board vote with Potter to dissolve the small lending institution, so needed by Bedford Falls' working classes, George sacrifices his desires and dreams so others may live in a small home with four walls and a bath, thus saving many from spending their lives in Potter's slums. George even helps out Iris Bick, risking his own reputation as small town tongues wag. But George does not realize how much good he has done. Without George, the lovely, peaceful hamlet of Bedford Falls would have devolved into Potterville, a tawdry, bar-filled, hard town, filled with unhappy and sullen people.

The man behind the chair remains silent as his boss rakes George over the coals. With a word, this unknown, unnamed man could have saved George a great deal of anguish, pain, and suffering. But, like Pilate, he washes his hands of the matter, and George heads for the bridge.

The movie opens with people's prayers, and now George stops at Martini's restaurant and voices a prayer: "Lord, I'm not a praying man, but show me the way" (sidenote: the movie originally ended with the whole crowd in the Bailey living room kneeling and praying the Lord's Prayer, but Capra cut the scene due to time constraints [see Basinger 1986]). George mistakenly thinks the answer to his prayer is the immediate response, a punch in the jaw from Mr. Welch. Bleeding at the mouth, George heads out into the blinding snow, crazed and a bit drunk, planning to end his life in the dark, cold swirling river waters.

Again the habits of a lifetime of helping others inspire George to dive in to save Clarence. And in helping one another, all is saved. George goes through a period of uncomfortable growth in self-awareness. He struggles to comprehend the gift he has been given, the chance to see the world as if he had not been born. The truth explodes in his consciousness, and from Clarence's mouth, "You really had a wonderful life."

Mary Hatch-Bailey is the real hero of the story. As a child she swore she would love George forever, and that love sustains and saves her husband, her family, and the town. Instead of descending into self-pity and anger as her husband breaks down, she scatters all over town, telling people George is in trouble. All those George has helped over the years come to his aid.

As those inspired by the Holy Spirit, we should ponder where and how we should speak. We want to be like Mary, scattering all over town, telling people the good news that in helping one another we are set free. We don't want to remain mute, allowing the Potters of this world to take it all and leave the George Baileys tortured and torn.

So much and so many in our world call for us to get out from behind the chair and let the Potters know we will no longer cooperate with their malicious machinations. There is a lot to speak out about. Always being able to fund wars but not education; tax cuts for the rich and corporations while middle- and lower-class folk foot society's bills; the ongoing insanity of the wars in Iraq and Afghanistan; the low-grade horror of the destruction of our planet by soulless corporations obliterating our lands and waters. Just come to northeast Pennsylvania and New York's Catskill Mountains to check out the implications of fracking the Marcellus Shale for natural gas (http://abclocal.go.com/wpvi/story?section=news/ special_reports&id=7596610). The Delaware River provides water for fifteen million people. See the documentary *Gasland*, winner of the 2010 Sundance Film Festival (http://www.gaslandthemovie.com).

Read Nicholas Kristof and Shirley WuDunn's *Half the Sky: Turning Oppression into Opportunity Worldwide* (2009). The *New York Times* reporter and his wife argue that the nineteenth century saw the abolition of slavery and in the twentieth century humanity rejected totalitarianism. The challenge for the twenty-first century is the establishment of true and full equality for women. "More girls have been killed in last 50 years precisely because they were girls, than all the men who died in all the battles of the 20th century" (Kristof and WuDunn 2009, xvii). There are some one to three million (some estimates go as high as twenty-seven million) persons in literal slavery today on our planet, mostly women enslaved by sex traffickers (Kristof and WuDunn 2009, 9). The husband and wife authors provide four steps you can take in the next ten minutes to respond to the issues. (1) Go to www.globalgiving.org or www.kiva.org and open an account. (2) Sponsor a girl through Plan International, Women for Service, World Vision, or American Jewish World Service. (3) Sign up for womensensenews.org and worldpulse.com. (4) Join the CARE Action Network at www.can.care.org (Kristof and WuDunn 2009, 251).

Vince Gallagher's *The True Cost of Low Prices: The Violence of Globalization* (Orbis, 2nd ed., 2013) demonstrates that our mission calls for great changes. His easy-reading analysis of the structural injustices and institutionalized violence of our times makes our crying out for a savior during Advent and Christmas all the more real and imperative. The coming of God into our world is good news for the many but disconcerting and challenging news for the few at the top of the heap who hoard all the goods and wealth. Nothing new there. It's as old as Mary's Magnificat: "He has cast down the mighty from their thrones and has lifted up the lowly. He has filled the hungry with good things and the rich he has sent away empty" (Luke 1:52-53).

Catholic social teaching is a rich treasure trove of analysis, principles, and ideas that can guide and sustain our mission efforts. Jesuit Pete Henriot's team's classic book *Catholic Social Teaching: Our Best*

Kept Secret (Orbis, 4th ed., 2003) succinctly summarizes the more than one hundred years of modern Catholic social teaching. The *Catechism* clearly states what our church teaches on social justice. Recall the quotations from the *Catechism* (see p. 70 above).

None of this is makes for a smooth and tranquil existence. Yet, whoever said being a follower of Christ would be easy? And most of us are neither Bill Gates nor Bill Clinton. Still, we can all do something. As the justly famous Jesuit Daniel Berrigan once said about all the injustice and inequality facing us, "No one can do everything. But everyone can do something. And the moral distance between doing something and doing nothing is momentous indeed" (cf. Berrigan 1981, 155).

Don't stand behind Potter's chair. Go and live a life of service and sacrifice like George Bailey. Go like Mary Bailey and spread the word that people are in trouble and ask people to help. Go and learn again the lesson taught many of us in first grade by the good sisters: It's better to be a giver than a taker. Be like Br. Dennis Ryan, S.J., not Bernie Madoff.

Know the truth of our faith: Our God gives himself so we can live. Let's undergo our metanoias, the turning of our hearts and minds to God, and live the truth of Christ, the truth embroidered beneath the picture of Peter Bailey in George's office: "All you can take with you is that which you give away."

Here in the United States we are grossly misappropriating our common funds. The American Friends Service Committee had a campaign to raise as much as the U.S. military spends in a minute: 1.2 million dollars. Yes, in the time it takes you to read this page the military machine will have blown some 2.4 to 3.6 million bucks. Dwight D. Eisenhower, the soldier who led the assault on D-Day in 1944 and went on to become president, said, "Every gun that is made, every warship launched, every rocket fired, signifies in the final sense a theft from those who hunger and are not fed, those who are cold and are not clothed" (American Friends Service Committee. www.oneminuteforpeace.org).

The Budget of the USA

57% on the military; 43% on everything else

57.0%	Military
05.5%	Veterans Benefits
06.0%	Education
06.0%	Government
05.5%	Housing and Community
05.0%	Health
04.0%	International Affairs
03.0%	Energy and Environment
02.5%	Science
02.5%	Labor
02.0%	Transportation
01.0%	Food and Agriculture

Source: American Friends Service Committee

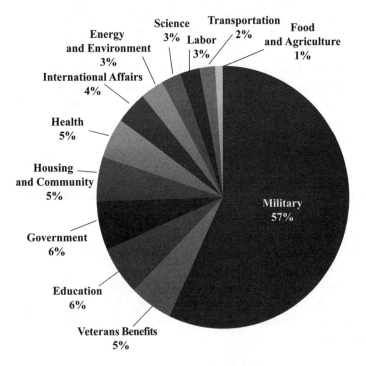

Source: American Friends Service Committee

Jesuit priest John Dear has been a tireless and selfless apostle for peace: he has written more than twenty books and hundreds of articles and talks, and he has been arrested dozens of times. John has spent his life trying to get the world to realize that Jesus wants us to reconcile and make peace with one another. He preaches that God calls us to end war. Dear has received many awards and recognitions, most notably Archbishop Desmond Tutu's nominating him for the Nobel Peace Prize. Tutu wrote:

> [John Dear] is the embodiment of a peacemaker. He has led by example through his actions and in his writings and in numerous sermons, speeches and demonstrations. He believes that peace is not something static, but rather to make peace is to be engaged, mind, body and spirit. His teaching is to love yourself, to love your neighbor, your enemy, and to love the world and to understand the profound responsibility in doing all of these. He is a man who has the courage of his convictions and who speaks out and acts against war, the manufacture of weapons and any situation where a human being might be at risk through violence. Fr. John Dear has studied and follows the teachings of nonviolence as espoused by Mahatma Gandhi and Martin Luther King, Jr. He serves the homeless and the marginalized and sees each person as being of infinite worth. I would hope that were he to receive this honor his teachings and activities might become more widely accepted and adopted. The world would undoubtedly become a better and more peaceful place if this were to happen. (wikipedia.org/wiki/John_Dear)

Let's go and be like Dennis Ryan and George Bailey. Let's go and be like Dorothy Day, Daniel Berrigan, and John Dear. Let's be like John Paul II, Mother Teresa, and Pope Francis. Come on. We're going to change the world.

CHAPTER 9

Practice Makes Us Better, Not Perfect

There's a wideness in God's mercy, like the wideness of the sea; there's a kindness in his justice, which is more than liberty.
—Traditional Hymn

There are very few men who realize what God would make of them if they abandoned themselves entirely to His hands, and let themselves be formed by His Grace.
St. Ignatius of Loyola, Rome, April 25, 1543

God doesn't love the poor because the poor are good. God loves the poor because God is good.
—Dean Brackley, S.J.

It was 1961. Kennedy was president and John XXIII was pope. A middle-aged Italian man who lived on the outskirts of Rimini, Italy, went to the local church for confession. When the priest slid open the panel in the confessional, the man said: "Bless me, Father, for I have sinned. . . . It's been many years since my last confession. During World War II, a beautiful Jewish woman from our neighborhood knocked urgently on my door and asked me to hide her from the Nazis. So I hid her in my attic." The priest replied, "That was a courageous thing you did, and you have no need to confess that." "There is more to tell, Father. . . . Well we were young and lonely and the world was in turmoil. And we turned to one another for comfort,

. . . uh, physical comfort. This happened several times a week, and sometimes twice on Sundays." The priest said, "Well, the two of you were in great danger and under great stress. Two people under those circumstances can easily succumb to the weakness of the flesh. However, if you are truly sorry for your actions, you are indeed forgiven." "Thank you, Father. That's a great load off my mind. I do have one more question." "And what is that?" asked the priest. "Do I have to tell her the war is over?"

Becoming a Catholic on fire with the power of the Holy Spirit is a process. It sometimes takes years to get things in order in our lives. Being a Catholic is not a competition. Going to Mass every Sunday doesn't make you a winner in some kind of cosmic game show over someone who misses Mass regularly. But going to Mass at least once a week, praying consistently, finding ways to serve others, not just at Thanksgiving and Christmas time, will most likely make you more happy and healthy and holy and free than if you are lackadaisical or slothful in the practice of the faith.

Jesus teaches "Be perfect as your heavenly Father is perfect" (Matt 5:48). The Greek word translated "perfect" is *telos* from which we get words like "teleological." Jesus is actually saying "be complete," "be fulfilled," as your heavenly Father is complete and fulfilled. It means being perfect the way a great work of art is perfect, that is, by being perfected, completed. The way a perfect game in baseball means twenty-seven batters up and twenty-seven batters down, with not even one batter reaching first base. Living the teachings of Jesus as a Catholic will complete and fulfill us. The meaning of the word "perfect" has come to mean too wearying a striving for an unattainable *ideal*. Being Catholic is all about doing the possible and leaving the rest to God. "Jesus did not believe in the perfecting of the human. . . . Jesus believed not in the constant 'improvement' of human beings but that the people of God could all help one another, repeatedly forgive one another, and show one another the way" (Lohfink 2012, 356).

We don't have to, nor can we, achieve such completion or fulfillment alone. God comes to help us in and through the practices of our faith, especially the sacraments. The Catholic faith is an incarnational belief system. In the Eucharist, we touch our God. St. Ignatius teaches at the end of his thirty days of the full Spiritual Exercises that "love ought to manifest itself more by deeds than by words" (*Spiritual Exercises* §231). To be Catholic, to allow the fire of the Holy Spirit to burn within us, we need to reflect on the practices of our lives, the things we most often and habitually do. Our ways, both personal and social, of choosing, doing, and being form us into the persons we will be for all eternity. We form our habits and our habits form us.

Our faith teaches that human beings are basically good and that certain practices or habits can develop in us virtues, the consistent ability to act in a certain manner. Most little boys don't like baths, but if they don't learn to shower every day by the time they are thirteen, not many people will want to sit near them. Boys need to get into the practice of daily bathing. My dentist tells me I don't have to floss all my teeth; just the ones I want to keep. Attending Mass regularly, personal prayer, and service on behalf of justice are practices that remind us who and what we are in relation to God and others and form the cultural backbone of the Catholic faith.

If the ways we choose to live are filled with ethical and loving practices of service and self-sacrifice, of prayer and peacemaking, of life making and loving, our world will become more and more like the kingdom Jesus preached. If the ways we choose to live are filled with unethical and unloving ways of looking out for number one, of filling our heads and hearts with endless, mindless crap (e.g., the viewing of thousands of hours of mind- and heart-numbing television), of avoiding the real risk of loving and therefore never really living, the kingdom Jesus wants to give us will remain unnoticed, unwrapped, and unexamined.

Three areas many people find difficult to incorporate into the practices of their lives are the Catholic faith's teachings on economic matters, sexual behavior, and inclusion. All three become a bit more radical and attractive when we look at both areas and ask, "What is just here? What is the right and loving thing to do?"

Practicing Just Economic Ways of Being. In 2011, here in the United States, 46.2 million people were living below the poverty line of $23,021 for a family of four. That was 15 percent of the population (15.2 percent in 2010 but 11.3 percent in 2000). 16.1 million children (21.9 percent of children in America) were living in poverty. 7.6 million children (9.7 percent) did not have health insurance. The total number of people without health coverage is 46.8 million. Median Family Income in the United States in 2011 was $50,054. And there were significant differences among various census groupings. Median family income for Asians/PI, $65,129; for whites, $55,412; for Latinos, $38,624; for blacks: $32,229 (U.S. Census 2012).

The four hundred richest people in the United States have more net worth than the bottom 50 percent of the population of some three hundred million. America's top 1 percent hold more wealth than the 90 percent at the bottom. From 2002 to 2007, the top 1 percent got 65 percent of the economic gains of the period (Kristof 2011). This so-called Bush Expansion era would more aptly be called the five years when Bush and his buddies ripped off the country. As Bush left office, his Secretary of the Treasury, Henry Paulson, took a few pages to Congress and said the banks needed to be bailed out to the tune of $750 billion. The bankers and Wall Street got theirs. The rest of us are still trying to recover. The top 1 percent win, the rest of us lose (see Stiglitz 2013a).

Nobel Prize–winning economist Joseph Stiglitz argues that the tax system is "stacked against the 99 percent." The richest four hundred taxpayers, whose average annual income is $200 million, pay less than 20 percent in taxes. "116 of the top 400 earners . . . paid less than 15 percent" (think Mitt Romney and his 14-percent tax bill). General Electric pays less than 2 percent. Stiglitz writes, "Neither G.E. nor Mr. Romney has, to my knowledge, broken any tax laws, but the sparse taxes they've paid violate most Americans' basic sense of fairness." The tax code gives big rewards to politicians' campaign contributors in the form of tax breaks for those who own things like "vacation homes, racetracks, beer breweries, oil refineries, hedge funds and movie studios, among many other favored assets or indus-tries" (Stiglitz 2013b).

Almost half the world—over three billion people—live on less than $2.50 a day. The GDP (Gross Domestic Product) of the forty-one most heavily indebted poor countries (567 million people) is less than the wealth of the world's seven richest people combined. Nearly a billion people entered the twenty-first century unable to read a book or sign their names. Less than 1 per cent of what the world spent every year on weapons was needed to put every child into school by the year 2000. We failed to stop the spending on war and switch the funds to education. One billion children live in poverty (roughly one in two children in the world). 640 million live without adequate shelter, 400 million have no access to safe water, 270 million have no access to health services. 10.6 million died in 2003 before they reached the age of five (or roughly 29,000 children per day). http://www.globalissues.org/article/26/poverty-facts-and-stats).

Despite present inequalities, some progress has been made in recent decades. The challenge is to continue to see that things improve rather than slip back into more gross inequality. Poverty was radically reduced in recent decades. Among other places, China was starving in the twentieth century. In 1929, 2 million died and in 1958-1961, some 23 to 40 million died from lack of food in China. The World Bank reports that the percentage of people in the developing world living on less than $1.25 a day was 20.6 percent in 2010, down from 43.1 percent in 1990 and 52.2 percent in 1981. That means 1.22 billion people in 2010 were living on less than $1.25 a day, down from 1.94 billion in 1981. Still, "Notwithstanding this achievement, even if the current rate of progress is to be maintained, about 1 billion people will still live in extreme poverty in 2015" (World Bank 2013).

Being Catholic means getting educated about these matters and doing what one can in response. Prayerfully considering the grow-ing income inequality in the United States and the radically unequal distribution of goods by corporate capitalism calls us to apply the teachings of Jesus and change things. It's all about relationships, our relationship with God and our relationships with others. If we saw all as our kin, much would change. The lack of family style and the inhumane machinations of corporate capitalism are also having a perverse effect on our most intimate relations. When every relationship is seen through the lens of cost-benefit analysis, we see our most intimate relations reduced to mere things to be consumed without meaning, or love.

Practicing Sane and Loving Sexuality. Notre Dame sociologist Christian Smith and his colleagues have been chronicling the experiences of young or emergent adults for the past few decades (Smith and Snell 2009; Smith et al. 2011). They note trends among, and question practices of, young men and women in the United States' mainstream culture, especially college culture. They think that it is good for people to be able to think deeply about the moral implication of their choices but find too many of our young adults "morally adrift." They think it good that people not become addicted to the consumerist mentality but rather know why they hold the values and meanings to which they adhere. A "lifestyle of routine intoxication" is deficient, and they warn that too many young adults accept the black-out style of drinking and drugging as all too normal. Sexual practices devoid of commitment, or even deep personal relationship, that is, the hook-up culture, are the norm for a large number of young adults, and too many have no real awareness of sex as a good connected to the choice to procreate and normed by appropriate and life-enhancing boundaries. Smith and his fellow researchers find young adults overall having too little interest in, or awareness of, the larger political, social, and cultural worlds surrounding and affecting them (Smith et al. 2011, 8-11). My mission field is the imaginations of young adults. I resonate with Smith and his colleagues' findings.

"Fr. Malloy, are you a virgin?" So inquired an undergrad in my Intro to Sociology class. Every semester, usually just before fall or spring break, I hand out 3 x 5 index cards and tell the students, "We've been studying religion as an institution in society. Here's your chance to ask a Jesuit priest anything you ever wanted to ask.

Go ahead. Write down your question. Don't sign your name. No topic is off limits."

The questions run the gamut from "Do you really believe God exists?" and "Why is there so much suffering in the world?" to "If you Jesuits take a vow of poverty, where do you get your money?" and "We know you're really the Exorcist for the diocese. C'mon, you can tell us. Why can't you tell us?" To the last one I reply, jokingly, "I would tell you, but then I'd have to kill you!" The undergrads often ask, "Why can't women be priests?" (The anthropological and sociological implications of the issue are uneven across various cultures. Some would accept women priests, many would not), and "Why can't priests get married?" (Actually there are dozens of married priests in the United States, previous Protestant ministers who have converted to Catholicism). Invariably, I get a smattering of questions about my sex life (I try and tell them I have a life filled with relationships, not a sex life). "Did you ever have a girlfriend?" (I reply, "Yeah. Lots. And Julia Roberts went home and cried herself to sleep when she learned I was entering the Jesuits. I really hated to break her heart, but God called and . . ."").

The "Are you a virgin?" question, however, was new. It gave me a chance to speak about sex and intimacy in ways I realized my students have never heard. In many ways, I found myself responding to Julia Tier's "Sex and the University," a sensitive and honest article about being at Mass one Sunday evening and realizing what she and many others in the chapel had been doing the night before. She writes:

> In my experience many women find one night stands emotionally unfulfilling and often hurtful. If the Church condemned this act because it is empty and damaging to all involved, I think a lot of young people would listen. It would certainly speak to their experience. Some might argue that this concern for our own dignity as well as our partners is, in fact, at the heart of the Church's wisdom on sexual matters. If so, at the age of 21, after 17 years of Catholic school, I've yet to hear it expressed in that way. Instead, young people are taught the act itself is wrong, which is often the only rewarding part. Until young Catholics

are provided with a sexual ethic that reflects their experience, rather than what they perceive to be an ironclad list of unjustified rules, they will continue to make decisions about sexuality without religion as an authority. (Tier 2004)

Tier and the students in my classes will not accept the message "sex is bad" when their experience tells them sex is the closest thing they can get to achieving real connection with another. The problem isn't sexual immorality so much as it is the inability of young adults to really relate to one another in ways that makes us all grow happy and healthy and holy and free. And it's not just hoary old celibates that are preaching this. Many worry about the effects of cell phones on young adults' abilities to communicate. They can text, but they can't talk. Real conversation frightens them. So sex without conversation or real connection becomes the norm.

Notre Dame sociologist Christian Smith reveals that all is not well for the sexual ethic of "anything goes/do it in the road" (or Oval Office—this generation's model was Bill Clinton . . .). "Some recent accounts of young adult sexual behaviors seem to want to suggest in contrast to our story, that all is indeed well. Some writers celebrate young women's sexual license as a way to cheer on the alleged evening of the old double standard" (Smith et al. 2011, 149). Smith hears some say that as long as sex is "safe and consensual," there's no problem. But research does not bear out this optimistic reading of the situation. "We raise doubts because we have heard too much directly from the mouths of emerging adults themselves about the major pain and damage that their free pursuit of sexual pleasure has often caused in their lives" (Smith et al. 2011, 150).

Catholicism must be presented to young adults not as "A Faith That Condemns" but as "A Faith That Frees" (a shameless Colbertian plug for my first book, I know). Too many YACs (Young Adult Catholics) hear only the negative about the church's teaching on sex and sexuality. We need to lead with the positive, challenging teens and "twenty-somethings" to strive for integration and intimacy. The church teaches chastity, the integration of sexuality into our lives

(CCC §2348). The church does not preach "Don't do it." The church preaches, "Have sex in a committed sacramental relationship, and experience the depths and joys of really relating and living in love over time." There are few human achievements as beautiful and meaningful as a fiftieth wedding celebration. The vast majority of people want to find one person and build a life with that loved one forever.

As the students warm to the topic, I go on: "For many of you, whether or not someone is a virgin is just a question about whether they have had sexual intercourse. Sex on the physical level alone is so much less than that to which persons are invited. The real question is whether one achieves intimacy in their relationships with others. Know that one can enjoy much intimacy without having sex." I continue, "You've been programmed to think you want a lot of sex, when what you truly and deeply desire is real and lasting, true and trusting, intimacy between yourself and another person. Intimacy is being at one with yourself so you can give yourself fully and freely, so you can unite yourself in love with another person. Simply having sex, like some proverbial rabbit, leaves you feeling unfulfilled and empty, because such sex is devoid of intimacy and integration. The danger of too much meaningless sex as a young person is that such free and supposedly easy hooking up makes it difficult to have truly meaningful sexual relations later in life. Sex without real, intimate connection may be a pleasant experience, but it fails to lead persons to transcendence, the going beyond ourselves to become who and what we truly desire to be, that which we are created to be, that is, lovers. Opening yourself and disciplining yourself to achieve and receive the grace of intimacy is a much more soul-satisfying way to live your life."

Along with poverty and obedience, Jesuits take a vow of celibate chastity. "Chastity means the successful integration of sexuality within the person" which leads to "inner unity" in both our body and spirit (CCC §2337). We all are called to be chaste, integrated, and loving, whether we are having sex or not. To know if you're sex life is chaste, integrated, and loving, ask yourself a simple question: "Do my sexual choices demonstrate justice?"

At this point my students are still attentive and listening, but the justice idea just sprained their brains. The wrinkled brows and questioning eyes communicate that they're with me but not understanding. They are wondering, "What the hell does justice have to do with sex?" Justice is the virtue of establishing right relationships. Sex, like everything else in our lives from economic activity to family relationships, must be engaged in justly, in ways that make our and others' lives happy and healthy and holy and free. You owe your partner in a sexual relationship what you owe anyone else in any relationship, that is, that which is their due. As those called to transformation in Christ, we owe it to one another to understand sex as a relational reality between persons, not as a meeting of things.

Students in a hyper individualist, crassly consumerist culture often look at sex the way they look at other "things." For those who are unreflective, sex can be just another meal in the "fast food" mall of life. Sex, seen as a thing one "gets," makes physical copulation like other products: one does and "gives" as little as one can to "get" as much as one can (students also look at course grades this way, but that's for another discussion . . .). Such a diminished philosophy of sex, leads to the using of one another for self-gratification. Then sexual intercourse devolves into an elaborate exercise in mutual masturbation. Sociologist Katie Bogle, in her study of student sexuality, notes that the hooking-up script calls for sex without strings, sex with no lasting connection (Bogle 2007). Such a script dictates that sex be anything but what it ought to be, that is, the intimate meeting of two persons in love and justice.

Margaret Farley in her magisterial book *Just Love: A Framework for Christian Sexual Ethics* locates love in real relationships and challenges us to live our sexual lives with others, according to the norms of justice. Farley writes,

> I propose a framework that is not justice *and* love, but justice *in* loving and in the actions that flow from that love. The most difficult question to be asked in developing a sexual ethic is not whether this or that sexual act in the abstract is morally good, but rather, when is sexual expression appropriate, morally good and just in a relationship of any kind. (Farley 2007, 207)

One student's critique of our freshmen orientation program was that there was no time devoted to sex education, although the incoming freshmen were subjected to skits warning of the dangers of date rape, and endless litanies about alcohol abuse's devastating effect on first year GPAs. What he meant by his complaint was that there was no instruction about the nuts and bolts of sex. Actually, all our "higher" education should take sex and intimacy education into account. Philosophy and theology courses should inculcate in young adults the habits of critical thinking necessary to meet the exigencies of our morally confusing age (as have all ages so been). Social science courses should be informing students about how relationships of all kinds (political, economic, educational, familial, and religious) interact with sexual acts and the meanings of those acts. Most importantly, the rules and regulations on campus ought to communicate clearly to students what is, and is not, acceptable and honorable behavior in matters sexual. We should be inviting our students to be their best selves in college. *Animal House*'s Deltas need not apply. Bluto Blutarski and his brothers Otter, Pinto, and Flounder go through college not only "drunk, fat, and stupid," but also infantile, insincere, and insecure. If that's what you want, there are plenty of schools out there willing to take your money and let you party while they laugh all the way to the bank. Catholic colleges ought to be environments wherein young adults are encouraged to discover who they truly are and desire themselves to be.

In romantic relationships, as in all relationships, power pulsates through and conditions choices. When power meets power, conflict erupts. When power meets vulnerability, oppression ensues. When vulnerability meets vulnerability, intimacy blooms. Too many sexual relationships are power games, contests those weaker, whether female or male, often lose. Instruction on how to avoid the inhumanity we can all too often inflict on one another, and how to foster the freeing and faithful interpersonal dynamics we all deeply desire and ultimately want, will go far in helping students to discover in themselves the courage and wisdom to navigate the wild waters of young adulthood. That's so much more than mere "sex ed."

I've spent almost twenty years teaching anthropology and sociology to undergrads. I've lived in a freshman dorm the past ten years. In thousands of conversations, often late at night (you gotta be in the student center at midnight to hear what is really going on), I've heard over and over the yearning young adults have for honest and life-giving relationships. The sad fact is that too many of today's young people are culturally conditioned to kneel down for oral sex or offer themselves on the contemporary altars, that is, beds, before such relationships can be born, nurtured, and allowed to grow. We shouldn't so much tell students to abstain from sex. We should say, "Sex, like an important athletic contest, demands training and coaching. You don't go to the Olympics without years of coaching and preparation. Sex is a lot more important than the Olympics." The church can coach young people in their sexual activities, and young adults are deeply desirous of such coaching. Those of us who dare to coach ought to also realize that in matters sexual, as in baseball, errors are part of the game. We coach gingerly and gently in the wake of the clergy sex scandals, realizing that as a group, we cannot automatically promote representatives of the institutional church as paragons of virtue. Better to admit we too are sinners called to follow Christ. Especially in a world where human bodies are ready for sex at age twelve, and social practices mean that people will not marry until their late twenties, we need to sculpt and promulgate programs that help young adults understand and embrace the practice of chastity.

A Catholic education ought to be about intimacy and integration and answering the eternal question "What is love?" Too few young adults know that the church's teaching on sex is about wholeness and integration, that is, chastity. All they have heard is that the church loudly says "NO!" while wagging a pointed finger. The truth is that the church says "Yes!" to truly transformative love and life-giving sex. Sex and all else that is holistically human and thus deeply divine ought to be for love, for true and lasting love. Love demands all of us. That's why marriage is a sacrament. Fifty years of marriage mediates grace to all involved. Parenting means twenty years and beyond of constant concern for a child. Sex demands true and ultimate concern for another person; thus the church teaches that sex be reserved for marriage. Sex as an expression and logical consequence of committed love is much more like prayer than it is like a simple bodily function. When sex resembles prayer there is a worshipful silence about the encounter. Silent and listen are spelled with the same letters. Let's challenge and help our young people to slow down, be quiet, and listen with their hearts to hear the deeper and challenging message of Jesus. Hopefully, we will all learn to discern the whisperings of God in our relationships, and then we will again discover love.

Love is what it's all about. And all real love requires sacrifice. Sacrifice means giving, letting another have what you could just as easily hold onto. Parents sacrifice daily and through a lifetime so their children can have what they need. From diapers and bicycles to braces and college tuition, and beyond, parents just give and give to their children. Love demands our giving our all.

There's a joke about a bishop who wants to go hiking. So he and a priest head out to Yellowstone for the day. The bishop tells priest to go up ahead. He'd like some quiet time alone. The priest comes upon a mother and a small child. He says hello and moves on ahead of them. All of a sudden a huge grizzly comes out of the woods and wants to eat the little kid. The priest gets between the bear and the mom and the child and says, "You can't eat the kid." The bear replies, "Look I'm really hungry and I need to eat something. I have low blood sugar. How about I eat the mom?" The priest says, "No way! That kid needs his mom." So the bear says, "OK, you're a priest. You don't have any kids. How about I eat you? Maybe some of your holiness would rub off on me too." The priest answers, "You're right, I don't have any kids. But really, I'm not all that holy. Look, why don't you wait five minutes. You can have the bishop."

Real love, true love, is all about sacrifice. The joke works on the fact that we should sacrifice for one another. The priest being willing to sacrifice the bishop is funny precisely because the priest is unwilling to sacrifice himself, as we would expect he would or should.

A couple of years ago I was at a family reunion and was deputized on a rainy, muggy summer day to take the bigger kids to a movie. So I and one of the dads motored over to the mall with the tweens and teens. The theater was big, air-conditioned, and comfy. We were going to see *Captain America*. I'm expecting nothing more than a fun summer movie: good guys, bad guys, a pretty girl, things blowing up. Based on the old Marvel comic books, Captain America is the story of Steve Rogers (Chris Evans), a skinny little guy who can't get into the army because he can't pass the physical. He desperately wants to fight the bad guys and make the world a better place. He finally gets into the army under a special program being run by a colonel (Tommy Lee Jones) and a scientist (Stanley Tucci), who are searching for a candidate to be scientifically altered to become Captain America.

Steve Rogers is running around a basic training facility with a couple of dozen football and lacrosse player types, big, strong guys, the kind who are athletically gifted and too often know it. They look down on skinny Steve and heap verbal abuse on him. Out of this crowd, Captain America will be selected.

One day, the colonel takes a grenade, pulls the pin and rolls the pineapple looking object into the midst of the candidates. All the Lax players and football types scatter like scared rabbits. Skinny Steve Rogers throws himself on the grenade, fully expecting to be blown to bits. On realizing the grenade is not exploding, he looks up in amazement and says, "What is this? Some kind of test?" The colonel and the scientist exchange knowing looks. They have found their man.

The night before he goes into the machine to be changed into Captain America, the scientist has a talk with Steve Rogers. He explains to Steve why he was chosen. Steve's willingness to sacrifice himself for others was the indication that he had what it takes to be trusted with the power he will receive as Captain America.

The rest of the movie was good guys, bad guys, a pretty girl, and things blowing up. But I was blown away at this core Christian message, the central truth about love as sacrifice, being broadcast on movie screens across the country and world. The willingness to sacrifice for others is central to the transformation of our lives and of our societies.

Practicing Inclusion.   Love isn't just about sacrifice and giving. Love also demands our opening our hearts and our lives to others, even those seemingly very different from ourselves and "our" group(s).

Love calls us to practice inclusion. In June 2013, Marquette theologian Fr. Bryan Massingale gave a talk to leaders of American Jesuit Universities and Colleges. He argued that the church must become more inclusive. By 2033 there will be no majority group in the United States. In 2013, minorities constitute 34 percent of the U.S. population, while "whites" make up 65 percent. Children are more likely to be from minority groups. In June 2013, the U.S. Census noted that there are now more white deaths than births. Millennial Catholics, those born after 1981, are 39 percent white, 54 percent Hispanic and 3 percent black. Some 40 percent of whites between the ages of twenty-five and twenty-nine are college graduates. Only 23 percent of blacks and 15 percent of Latinos hold college degrees (Massingale 2013).

Until early in the twenty-first century, many among Catholics in the United States consciously or unconsciously thought of the church in terms of white culture and white ways of being. The fact of the matter is that now "the majority of U.S. Catholics are non-Anglos. When new members join the club, the club changes. This is not political correctness. This is the Gospel" (Massingale 2013).

For many in the United States, the church is still unconsciously thought of as an institution rooted in, and expressive of, European and North American tastes and sensibilities. Practicing inclusion will mean changing our mind-sets and cultural assumptions in the rapidly changing global community and communities within which "we live and move and have our being" (Acts 17:28).

A self-appointed Catholic watchdog once approached me and somewhat belligerently demanded if I preach a "Solid Catholicism." I answered, "No." He was suitably shocked. I told him I preach a full and flexible Catholicism. I don't want a "Solid Catholicism" if a "Solid Catholicism" means an intolerant, judgmental Catholicism. I don't want a "Solid Catholicism" if that means a fundamentalist Catholicism. I don't want a fundamentalist Catholicism any more than any sane and good Muslim wants a fundamentalist Islam. Simplistic, self-evident religious truths too often are used by self-appointed, self-confident, self-righteous believers to pain and punish people who don't fit into contemporary Pharisees' narrow categories. Simplistic, self-serving interpretations of Holy Scripture too often are used to oppress and bludgeon people. Simplistic, narrow, unintelligent, and uninspiring reiterations of the Catholic tradition do not foster the love and freedom and justice that the sons and daughters of God need and deserve. For instance, the word in Romans 1 is not *porneia,* the Greek word the New Testament uses for sexual immorality, that is, fornication (Matt 5:32; 19:9; 1 Cor 6:9). Romans 1:26 refers to dishonorable passion (*pathe atimias*), not "homosexuality," as many understand the word today. St. Paul challenges unbridled lust and sexual perversion. It's a leap to say that St. Paul in the first chapter of Romans is speaking of what we mean by "homosexuality" in the twenty-first century.

Frankly, I want a fluid and flexible Catholicism. We baptize with water; we don't stone one another in initiation rites. And too much of the "Solid Catholicism" I hear today consists of casting stones at sinners, usually with a disproportionate amount of attention paid to homosexuals and abortionists, while neglecting to question the executives of the banks that needed a $750 billion bailout in 2008, the architects of continual and constant wars, or the CEOs of corporations that fashion a world of the very few fabulously rich and the vast majority of struggling middle class and the desperate poor. I want a Catholicism that is fluid and flexible and intelligent enough, and wide and broad enough, to address the issues of poverty and war and abortion and human sexuality. I want a Catholicism that welcomes and embraces sinners and calls sinners to conversion. I want a compassionate, challenging, and courageous Catholicism that is open, intelligent, and in dialogue with our world and our cultures. I do not want a "solid Catholicism" if that means a Catholicism that is intolerant, judgmental, rigid, simplistic, and oppressive. I want a Catholicism that liberates. I want a Catholicism that calls all of us to fashion a world of justice and peace, a world wherein we all can grow happy and healthy and holy and free.

Why? Why is a fluid and flexible Catholicism better than a "Solid Catholicism"?

First, Jesus was fluid and flexible. Jesus changed and challenged things religious. Jesus operated in a flexible and fluid manner in opposition to some of the Pharisees, those "Solidly Jewish" practitioners of his day.

Jesus was fluid and flexible before the Law. The book of Leviticus condemns all kinds of things. True, it says, "Do not lie with a male as with a woman" (18:22). But Lev 25:44 says, "It is from the nations around you that you may acquire male and female slaves." Does that justify our paying Mexicans slave wages today? Leviticus 21:5 says, Priests "shall not make bald spots upon their heads or shave off the edges of their beards." Leviticus 21:20 says that no priest may have any eye defect. So my glasses and less than full head of hair disqualify me from serving at the altar? Leviticus 24:19 states that if anyone injures his neighbor, whatever he has done must be done to him: "fracture for fracture, eye for eye, a tooth for a tooth." The injury inflicted is the injury to be suffered. I hope that doesn't get invoked if you're involved in an auto accident.

Jesus challenged the rigid and solid notions of the Jewish law in the name of the God he related to as Father, a God of love and mercy, a compassionate God who cares for and converts sinners, not a God who castigates and condemns those who succumb through human frailty to temptation and sin. Jesus doesn't condemn such people (i.e., all of us). Jesus saves and transforms us.

Second, Catholicism is fluid and flexible. Catholicism changes. The Catholic Church used to outlaw usury, that is, the lending of money at interest. The Catholic Church, as did all churches of the times, used to allow slavery. The Catholic Church, as did all churches of the time, used to segregate blacks and whites in the churches of the United States. In the 1930s and 1940s, when Jesuits like Horace McKenna and Dick McSorley began to integrate the Jesuit parishes of the southern Maryland counties, they were fiercely criticized and condemned. But by the end of World War II, FDR and Eleanor Roosevelt were calling for the integration of the Armed Forces, and Harry Truman so ordered integration of our military in 1948. The church changes the world and the world changes the church. By the 1950s and 1960s all churches were being challenged to accept blacks as full and equal members of their congregations. And Vatican II acknowledged that salvation could be realized beyond the rigid borders of institutional Catholicism.

Third, Catholicism must be in dialogue with culture. Catholicism cannot be in mindless opposition to culture. The church must be in the world and in dialogue with the world in order to call all to the truth and justice, peace and freedom, of God's kingdom. One cultural reality changing at warp speed these days is the reality of homosexuality in our world.

The *Catechism* says that homosexual acts are not approved (CCC §2357). As heterosexual acts outside of marriage are not approved, so too homosexual acts. The church further states homosexual acts are intrinsically disordered, as are many acts: lying, underpaying employees, cheating on tests. But the next paragraph states: "The number of men and women who have deep-seated homosexual tendencies is not negligible. They do not choose their homosexual condition. . . . They must be accepted with respect, compassion, and sensitivity. Every sign of unjust discrimination in their regard should be avoided" (CCC §2358). The *Catechism,* promulgated by John Paul II, says you cannot discriminate against gay people. We are all called to live chaste lives, both homosexuals and heterosexuals.

The church calls all to the ideal of reserving sex for married persons. The whole question of same-sex marriage is radically new. It was only in 1972 that the American Psychological Association deemed gays and lesbians "sane." Before that they were considered "mentally ill." For years I'd explain to undergrads that homosexual sex was illegitimate in the eyes of the church because, like heterosexual sex outside of marriage, it didn't express the fullness of a sacramental union. No one ever raised a hand and suggested that homosexuals should be allowed to marry. But with lightning speed, Iowa and some other states have allowed same-sex marriage, while California voted it down. Go figure: Iowa more liberal than California. All of society is experiencing tumultuous times around the issue. The church is facing something radically new here and, as always, moves slowly in such matters. What the church is advocating for is good and life-giving and life-sustaining sex, and such sex is more likely to occur in sacramental marriage. There is a lot of heterosexual sex that is demeaning and destructive (prostitution, human trafficking, "hooking-up"). There is a lot of homosexual sex that is demeaning and destructive (prostitution, human trafficking, and phenomena like sex on the "down low," where straight men have homosexual sex).

Andrew Sullivan, one of the most articulate and thoughtful proponents of changing the Catholic Church's practices toward gays, wrote in the *New York Times* a few years ago that he was leaving the church. As a gay man, he could no longer accept the intolerance and rejection he feels. I'd challenge the Mr. Sullivans of the church to stay, and stay in dialogue with the community. Two-thousand-year-old institutions like the Catholic Church, an institution of more than 1.2 billion members that span hundreds of cultures and countries, do not change rapidly. That's simply a social fact. I sometimes wish that things would change more quickly, but I also sometimes wish rainwater were beer. And the Mr. Sullivans of the world have to note that many in the church do struggle to accept and support gays and lesbians. The Vatican may have the final word, but it doesn't have the only word. And the word of the Vatican changes. Just look at altar girls, once prohibited, now commonplace. Pope Francis caused a stir when he said in a press conference on a plane returning from World Youth Day in Rio in 2013 that he didn't feel he was called to judge gay priests who are living celibate lives and seeking the Lord. The church, like all human institutions, changes slowly, but it does change. We all have to remain in dialogue with and within the culture of the church.

Remember things do change. We no longer allow people to legally own slaves. We no longer prevent the lending of money at interest. We no longer condemn our Jewish and Protestant and Muslim and Buddhist friends for believing and practicing a faith different from our own. Women can vote. An African American family resides and serves in the White House (maybe it's time to change the name of that residence? Maybe Rainbow House?).

A challenging, courageous, compassionate Catholicism is not easy. A "Solid Catholicism" is seemingly more clear and settled. A "Solid Catholicism" gives one the comfort of being "right," "correct," "orthodox." But Jesus never much applauded those who thought themselves righteous. Jesus values more those who are consistently and constantly loving. The open, shifting, fluid Catholicism I'm advocating may get all sides yelling at you. So be it. So they treated the prophets before us. Let's pray that our eyes are opened, the eyes of our hearts and minds, so that Jesus can show us the way.

By 2035 there will be 8 billion people on the planet and there will be no racial group in the United States that exceeds 50 percent of the population. We have moved from a world in which the Western nations dominated, to a world in which the United States was the predominant force, to a world of global connections and relationships among many powerful nations and even more powerful corporations. Financial markets are more and more centered in places like London rather than on Wall Street; the tallest building in the world is in Dubai and the world's richest person is no longer a citizen of the United States. (In June 2013 *Forbes* listed Mexican Carlos Slim Helu as having $73 billion to Bill Gates's $67 billion.) Bollywood has overtaken Hollywood as the major movie producer of the age. In 2008, only one of the top ten shopping malls in the world was in the United States. "The West" is seeing the arrival of "the Rest" on the scene, and European/North American cultural assumptions no longer rule the way we see the world, think about values and symbols, or do things. Some minions of the mass media in the United States make profits by demonizing "others" but do a grave disservice by implying that the world is much more dangerous and explosive than it really is. The false pontificating about the threat of Islamic terrorists misses the reality of the millions of Muslims living in the United States who neither want nor support the Bin Ladens of the world. Islamic terrorists are no more representative of Islam than those who murder abortionists are representative of Catholics in the United States. Muslims will make up only 5 to 8 percent of Europe by 2035, and support for suicide bombers and Al Qaeda is disappearing in most of the Muslim world. Facts are, we live in times of relative peace, certainly in comparison to most of the twentieth century (cf. Zakaria 2008).

Practicing an attitude of global inclusion will no longer simply mean "we" accept "them." "We" in the United States now need to be not only those who welcome but also those who realize that the many in the world welcome "us" as equal partners in conversation and power. The way we live our Catholic faith will be marked as much by Indian and African and Latin American and Asian cultural ways of knowing and being and doing as it is by European and North American cultural modes of life. One very concrete example of this is the need to accustom our ears as more and more priests from places like India and Africa preach in parishes on Sunday. Too many in the United States complain that they cannot understand the priest's accent. It is time to open our ears and develop the capacity to discern accents. For many Catholics, who cannot comprehend why the church won't change teachings on the ordination of women or homosexual marriage, the awareness that in places like Kenya and parts of Argentina such attitudes and desires are anathema may help temper impatience with the seemingly glacial pace of change in a global church. For those who want to go back to pre-Vatican II modes of worship and prayer, privileging Latin and archaic vestments, awareness that liturgy in Uganda and Sri Lanka not only cannot afford the liturgical accoutrements needed for such celebrations may help them realize the undesirability of forcing people to "return" or "restore" ways of worship they never knew nor now want.

Our practice of Catholicism can make us and our world better. We have come a long way. We have a long way to go. Let's enjoy the journey.

CHAPTER 10

Smile: Despite It All, the Universe Is User-Friendly

The Arc of the Moral Universe is long, but it bends toward Justice.
—Rev. Martin Luther King, Jr.,
sermon in the National Cathedral, March 31, 1968

But what about overall happiness? . . . More Americans describe themselves as happy today (82%) than any other self-description. The happiest of all? The young (Millennials, at 92%), the financially well-off (those earning over $60,000 annually, at 88%) and practicing Catholics (at 93%).
—Barna, "How the Last Decade Changed American Life"

Andrew S. Quinn, Esq., was an executive for a large medical services company. He wrote a report that infuriated one of the people evaluated. The man, a very vertically challenged person, stormed into Andy's office and with fists on hips loudly pronounced, "I'm not happy." Without missing a beat, Andy replied, "Well, then you must be Grumpy."

The basic principle and message of Catholicism is this: God loves us. So smile. Be happy. Our lives, with all the good and with all the bad, are basically wonderful and full of wonder, if we just allow our eyes to be opened and see. As a matter of fact, a much higher percentage of practicing Catholics report being happy in comparison to the general population in the United States (Barna 2013).

St. Ignatius teaches that the relationship between lovers consists in the mutual sharing of gifts. God gives us everything. We live in gratitude and a stance of being willing to share our gifts with others.

As a little boy climbed onto Santa's lap, Santa asked the usual, "And what would you like for Christmas?" The child stared at him open-mouthed and horrified for a minute, then gasped: "Didn't you get my e-mail?"

God wants to give us gifts. Do we send God an "e-mail"? Do we pray and converse with God about gifts received, gifts needed, gifts shared? Are we willing to change ourselves, our desires, our world, in order to receive such gifts? Are we able to see that God desires that all our brothers and sisters share in God's gifts?

Megan and her eight-year-old sister, Marcia, had been fighting a lot the past year. This happens when you combine a headstrong four-year-old and a ten-year-old sharing the same room. Megan's parents, trying to take advantage of Megan's deep yearly interest in Santa Claus, reminded the four-year-old that Santa was watching and doesn't like it when children fight. This had little impact. Megan and Marcia continued to battle all the time. "I'll just have to tell Santa about your misbehavior," the mother told Megan as she picked up the phone and dialed. Megan's eyes grew big as her mother said, "Hello. Mrs. Claus" (any parent knows how to dial Santa's house). Could she put Santa on the line? Megan's mouth dropped open as Mom described to Santa how the four-year-old was acting. When Mom said that Santa wanted to talk to her, Megan reluctantly took the phone. "Santa," in a deepened voice, explained to her how there would be no presents Christmas morning for children who fought with their siblings. Santa would be watching, and he expected things to be better from now on. Megan, now even more wide-eyed, solemnly nodded to each of Santa's remarks and silently hung up the phone when he was done speaking. After a long moment, Mom asked, "What did Santa say to you, dear?" In almost a whisper, Megan sadly but matter-of-factly stated, "Santa said he won't be bringing Marcia any toys this year."

To live our lives fully, to be happy and holy and healthy and free, to trust in our God no matter what happens, to be on fire, we need a gift. That gift, that grace, is faith. Grace is the power to do what you could not do before. When the hurricanes hit we need faith. When mass shootings and bombings happen, we need faith. When we're unemployed, we need faith. When someone we love dies, we need faith. We need to put on the garments of faith. When we were baptized we put on the white garments of salvation. We were clothed in faith. Speaking of garments . . . let me tell you about a jacket . . .

When I was five years old I wanted a Davy Crockett jacket. I believed I was going to get that jacket. I had faith. I knew Santa would get it for me. I'd seen him at Wanamaker's, the big department store in downtown Philly. We always met my grandmother at the huge bronze Eagle (the "Iggle" in Philadelphiaese) at the entranceway before going to see the Christmas Toyland display and Santa. I asked him for the jacket. That Christmas, I rushed to the tree on Christmas morning. No jacket. I was told the elves didn't make enough jackets that year. When I was six, I was told Santa wanted to wait to give me the jacket until I learned to remember to bring home things like sweatshirts and mittens I'd forget at the playground. When I was seven, I ran down on Christmas morning and . . . still no jacket. This time my mother said maybe there were other ways to get the jacket. That night, we went to Grandmom's. My grandmother gave me a heavy box. I tore off the shiny, red paper and saw it was from Wanamaker's. I figured a sweater or maybe a shirt. But I pulled out a beautiful, soft, chamois leather Davy Crockett jacket with all the fringe and a shiny, satin lining. It was the absolute best. I didn't take that jacket off for a week. I slept in it. I didn't want to take a bath because I'd have to take it off. I felt so cool with the tan leather fringe all up and down the arms of the jacket just like the hero of the Alamo.

First day back at school. Jimmy O'Leary. Big kid. He was mean and ugly and he smelled bad. I was in second grade; he was in fifth. I'd heard Jimmy had been kept back a couple of times. I think he was already shaving. We little kids tried to avoid him. He looked at my new jacket, came over, shoved me and sneered, calling me "Annie Oakley."

Now, when I was little, I was small. I was one of the younger kids in my class and was always at the front of the line, which went according to height. My buddies Frankie and Pat told me to let it go, that Jimmy would kill me if I did anything. But I was so mad. So, I did what any self-respecting Philadelphia Irish Catholic kid on the black asphalt parking lot school playgrounds of my youth would do. I ran over, swung from my heels, and punched Jimmy O'Leary right in the mouth. He bled all over the snow, and cried like a kindergartener. I felt great, for a second. But then I suddenly realized the whole world was going to end. Jimmy O'Leary was eventually going to get up and kill me. Safety Noreen Ryan, an eighth grader, came over and grabbed me and said, "Ricky Malloy, you're such a trouble maker. I'm going to take you to Sr. Teresa, . . . again." Noreen was such a goody, goody. But she saved me that time.

Sr. Teresa. The principal. Being taken to her office always felt like the end of the world. To a second grader like me, she seemed eight feet tall. She and I had had a lot of little "talks" in my first year and a half in school. She told me I was wild and unruly. She said I lacked discipline and self-control. She already had the ruler out. She never really hit me very hard. It was the whole ritual of the thing that made me know I'd really done something wrong.

She asked me what happened. This time I had a scathingly brilliant idea and came up with a really good excuse. I told her Jimmy O'Leary had made fun of my jacket and that in smacking him, I was really defending my grandmother, who had given me the jacket. Sr. Teresa, trying to suppress a smile, said, "Well I guess, if you were defending your grandmother, that constitutes extenuating circumstances." So I didn't get smacked with the ruler . . . that time. A couple of days later my mom was in the ACME, the supermarket in Philly, and Jimmy O'Leary's mom comes over and asks my mom where she can get a Davy Crockett jacket like mine for Jimmy. Jimmy had been making fun of something even he knew was cool and valuable.

What's all this have to do with faith? I learned when I was young I had to be willing to fight to defend the gifts I'd been given. Are we? Are we ready to struggle for the gift of faith we've been given, even when the Jimmy O'Learys of the world ridicule us, even when the terrors and trials, the disasters and deaths, the pulverizing pains and sheer sadness of human existence seemingly mock our beliefs? Years ago our parents and loved ones took us to church and dressed us in beautiful clothing, a white garment, as we were baptized into the faith of our community, the faith of our grandparents and ancestors all the way back to Mary and Joseph, to Miriam, Moses, and Zipporah, to Abraham and Sarah. Are we willing to struggle for that faith we were given? We are called to keep the faith, our Catholic faith, alive.

Faith is a way of knowing things you can't know any other way. I'm told I have DNA. I've never seen it, but I have faith it is in my cells. I have faith China exists, but I've never been there. Still, I firmly believe China is on the other side of the world. I don't think we're living in some "Truman Show" where reality is all contrived and based on a lie. On a deeper level of faith, faith that cannot be empirically verified, I believe God exists and loves us and gives us the Holy Spirit so we can be transformed in Christ (Rom 5:5).

This book is a call to go deeper into faith, an invitation to be set on fire with faith. The only way to do that is to practice the faith. Try going to daily Mass. Learn about and make St. Ignatius's daily Examen. Think about going on a silent retreat. Read the Gospels. Pray the Rosary. Get more involved in your parish. Watch *The Shawshank Redemption, It's a Wonderful Life, Places in the Heart,* and M. Night Shyamalan's *Wide Awake,* his little-known first movie, a moving tribute to a little boy's search for faith.

Faith is "the assurance of things hoped for, the evidence of things unseen" (Heb. 11:1). The world is troubled and we are called to transform and make our world better, more loving and more just. The world is always showing us that we need faith. Faith brings life to a world of disappointments, disillusionments, and disasters. Some see all the suffering and pain and say they don't believe in God. But there's still all the pain and suffering. It's people of faith who can respond to the suffering and pain. Given all the suffering and pain, it's a more interesting question to wonder why there is so much good. Horrific events, from tornadoes to mass shootings, bring enormous response in both material aid and spiritual support. Faith makes us able to notice and be grateful for all the good that exists despite so much evil.

The story began with Abraham believing God and Moses leading liberation. Prophets challenged kings. The world was transformed when an uneducated, poor Jewish girl gave a radical "Yes" to God's invitation. "And the Word became flesh and dwelt among us" (John 1:14). Jesus transformed all. Apostles were missioned. This is the start of the story of hope and healing, the way of love and liberty, the challenge of faith and freedom, given to us in Christ. "For freedom Christ has set us free" (Gal 5:1). This is our faith. Let's be willing to struggle for faith. Let's promote our faith. Let's be willing to pray for faith and then speak on behalf of faith. Let's be willing to live our faith. Watch out for the Jimmy O'Learys of the world, but don't let them extinguish the fire of our faith.

Our living our faith graces us with lives filled with meaning, purpose, and joy. Again, God wants to give us gifts. Do we really want to receive God's gifts? Better said, are we willing to be changed by our relationship with God? And are we willing to share our gifts with others? We experience peace and joy and happiness when we live lives on fire with the desire to help and serve others. Jesus once told a story about a Good Samaritan. If he told it today, it might go something like this.

An elderly woman is at a banquet hall at a town about five hours from her home where there are four or five wedding receptions going on. She is a well-to-do woman who takes great pride in being on top of things. She can take care of herself and is very angry with all these people who want to live off "welfare," even though the entitlement program AFDC (Aid to Families of Dependent Children) no longer exists and has been replaced by TANF (Temporary Aid to Needy Families), which can only be received for five years. She listens to a lot of Fox News. She thinks that if the government would just stop giving all these hand-outs, people would get off their butts and find jobs. And if the government would secure the borders, there wouldn't be all these Mexicans running around *making babies and getting a free ride from the government. And now she's annoyed. Why aren't there better signs around the place? Soon, she learns she's in the wrong place. She has to go to another banquet hall across town. She's upset. She had traveled alone and none of her friends or family had come with her. She has been having trouble with her bowels lately and feels the urgent need to use the bathroom. As she enters the ladies' room, a young woman, high on meth, slugs her in the face, snatches her purse, and runs. The woman screams. To make matters worse, the trauma causes her to soil herself. Her own excrement is spread all over her clothing and lower limbs. Now her clothes are a mess and she's crying for help. A priest walks by, but is late for a wedding reception at which he is to offer the grace before the meal. And there's no way a priest is going into the ladies' room. He ignores her cries. A well-dressed, rich woman emerges from a back stall and rushes past her. Her dress for the wedding is quite expensive and she doesn't want to get anything dirty on it. Besides someone will come and help the woman. She leaves the woman to fend for herself. The Mexican woman who cleans the bathrooms at the establishment comes to the woman's aid. She leaves her cleaning cart in the doorway and blocks access so the woman can have some privacy. She goes and gets a chair so the woman has a place to sit. She gets a washcloth and towel and helps the old woman get cleaned up. The Mexican woman goes to a Target store down the street and buys the woman underwear, stockings, shoes and a dress, all of which costs the Mexican woman more than $100, which is more than she earns in two days working at her $5.75 an hour job (the minimum wage, by law, is $7.25 an hour, but she's Mexican. How can she complain?) She borrows a cell phone from a fellow worker and calls the elderly woman's family, and then takes her to a local motel. She pays for a room for the night and lends the woman $50 dollars. She tells the maids, friends of hers, to keep an eye on the elderly woman and make sure she's okay. Who was a neighbor to the old woman?*

In Jesus' telling, the priest and Levite cannot help the beaten man for they would become ritually impure, in the same way that if you got excrement on yourself, you couldn't go to a wedding reception without washing up and changing your clothes first. The harder thing to grasp is how much animosity there was between Samaritan and Jew, an animosity that was both ethnic and religious. It would be like a Palestinian helping a Jew, or a black man helping a member of the KKK, a Tutsi in Rwanda helping a Hutu, or the brother of a murdered woman befriending the woman who killed her, as Ron Carlson forgave pick-axe murderer Karla Faye Tucker (see Arnold 2010, 86-91).

Ultimately, it's all about love. In a wonderful mystery novel by Yale law professor Stephen Carter, the main character Talcott Parsons says, "Love is an activity, not a feeling—didn't one of the great theologians say that? . . . True love is not the hapless desire to possess the cherished object of one's fervent affection. True love is the disciplined generosity we require of ourselves for the sake of another when we would rather be selfish" (Carter 2002, 215).

True love requires self-sacrifice and commitment. Just ask any parent. To be a Catholic, to be on fire for the faith, demands that we give our time and effort, our talents and treasure, our very self and soul, to the enterprise of being a practicing member of the church. It's like this old joke. A chicken and a pig were walking by St. Matilda's church and read the sign: "Prayer breakfast to raise money to save our school." The chicken said, "We should help out. We could donate the eggs and ham they need for the breakfast." The pig thought for a moment and replied, "Well, that's easy for you to say. For you that's a donation. For me it's a total commitment."

God makes a total commitment to us. God can save us from whatever mess we get ourselves into. God can save us from all the messes that rain on our lives, making our existence painful and seemingly unbearable. If God can save Louie Zamperini, God can save us all. If Louie Zamperini can forgive his tormentor and find peace, there's hope for all of us to work the reconciliations called for in our lives.

One of the most amazing stories describing the best and worst of humanity, and God's saving intervention in a man's life, is Laura Hillenbrand's *Unbroken*, her biography of Louie Zamperini. A 1936

Olympic runner, a World War II prisoner of war who suffered horrifically at the hands of a sadistic Japanese captor, and a man who triumphs over the horrors of PTSD (Post-Traumatic Stress Disorder) with the support of a loving and long-suffering wife and the conversion to Christ ignited by hearing the preaching of Billy Graham, Louie demonstrates that good can come from unbelievable evil. The love and commitment of Cynthia, his wife, sustained Louie as he struggled with self-destructive dynamics and abuse of alcohol as he strained to recover from having lived through forty-seven days adrift in a raft in the South Pacific after his plane went down, and then years in a POW camp. Louie was singled out for continual and horrendous abuse because he was a well-known Olympic runner. Louie suffered particularly brutal physical abuse, humiliation, debasement, and degradation at the hands of one guard, Mutshiro Watanabe, known as "the Bird." This sadistic guard took pleasure in persecuting, literally torturing, Louie, daily and persistently. When Louie refused to tape a message denouncing his country, he received even worse treatment. Louie and the other prisoners were constantly degraded and dehumanized.

> The guards sought to deprive them of something that had sustained them even as all else had been lost: dignity. This self-respect and sense of self-worth, the innermost armament of the soul, lies at the heart of humanness; to be deprived of it is to be dehumanized. . . . Men subjected to dehumanizing treatment experience profound wretchedness and loneliness and find that hope is almost impossible to maintain. Without dignity, identity is erased. (Hillenbrand 2010, 182-83).

On finally returning to the United States, Louie struggled to overcome the understandable difficulties he experienced in adjusting to normal life. Studies forty years after the war found that 85 percent of soldiers imprisoned in the Pacific experienced PTSD, 80 percent were psychiatrically impaired, and 60 percent had anxiety disorders. The suicide rate among former Pacific POWs was 30 percent greater than comparable groups (Hillenbrand 2010, 346-47).

In 1949, Cynthia dragged a resistant Louie to a Billy Graham crusade in Los Angeles. Something happened there that turned Louie's mind and heart and soul upside down and inside out. As he answered Graham's altar call, he experienced being back on the raft in the Pacific, and remembered a prayer he had lifted heavenward: "If you will save me, I will serve you forever" (Hillenbrand 2010, 375). After the powerful experience of Graham's crusade, Louie immediately quit drinking and his life resurrected. Louie's conversion is particularly notable for the manner in which he eventually came to forgive his persecutor, "the Bird." In 1950, Louie traveled back to Japan to try to meet his tormentor. In Sugamo prison in Japan, where those guards who had mistreated the American prisoners were incarcerated, Louie felt not hatred or anger at his captors. He experienced compassion and forgiveness for those who had treated him so horrifically. Years later, in 1997, his particular persecutor was located by CBS's Bob Simon, but Watanabe refused to meet with his former prisoner. In 1998, almost eighty-one years old, Louie carried a letter with him to Japan, expressing forgiveness for all that Watanabe had done to him and his fellow prisoners. Louie had traveled to Japan to carry the Olympic Torch and ran through the village of Naoetsu where he had suffered so much so many decades before. As the white-haired Louie trotted, "All he could see, in every direction, were smiling Japanese faces" (Hillenbrand 2010, 397).

In June 2012, Louie Zamperini, ninety-five years young, appeared on the *Tonight Show with Jay Leno*. Louie's energy and enthusiasm for life sparkling across the screen attest to the force and fire of faith, the deep strength of spirituality and the transformative power of forgiveness in the lives of believers. If someone like Louie can learn to trust and forgive and love after all he'd been through, there is hope for us all.

T. S. Eliot, the great twentieth-century poet, drew upon the well-known saying of the fourteenth-century mystic Julian of Norwich, and in his "Little Gidding," expresses well the ultimate promise of our faith.

Whatever we inherit from the fortunate
We have taken from the defeated
What they had to leave us—a symbol:
A symbol perfected in death.
And all shall be well and
All manner of thing shall be well
By the purification of the motive
In the ground of our beseeching.

(http://allspirit.co.uk/gidding.html)

Conclusion

A word from Charles Schulz's Peanuts: Lucy and Linus are look-ing out a window on a very rainy day. Lucy wonders if the whole world will ever flood again. Linus replies, "It will never do that. In the ninth chapter of Genesis God promised Noah that would never happen again, and the sign of the promise is the rainbow." Lucy smiles a wrinkly, happy smile and says, "You've taken a great load off my mind. . . ." Linus turns to Lucy and says, "Sound theology has a way of doing that."

The Good News of Christianity comes simply to this, that as a result of Jesus' death and resurrection we can now love God effec-tively only by loving one another. . . . Probably the greatest dif-ficulty with Christianity is that it is so utterly simple. The real novelty of the Christian gospel is the revelation that I must find God in Christ not "out there" and not merely "in here," in the sense of inside myself; I find Christ upon the faces and in the heart of humanity.

—Stanley, 1967, 228

Years ago in his study of Amerindian mythology, *The Raw and Cooked*, Claude Levi-Strauss analyzed human experience as sets of binary opposites. The good news is that our God bridges the differ-ence between God's and our being. As St. Athanasius said centuries ago, God becomes what we are, so we might become what God is. We get "cooked" by the Holy Spirit and are no longer "raw." We are transformed by the fire of the Trinity's love. We become fire. As those called to be Christ in the world today, we give light and heat, hope and love.

The great Jesuit philosopher and theologian Bernard Lonergan teaches that we are made for God, wired in such a way that the correct functioning of our minds and hearts leads us to fulfillment in God's being.

> Being in love with God is the basic fulfillment of our conscious intentionality. That fulfillment brings a deep-set joy that can remain despite humiliation, failure, privation, pain, betrayal, desertion. That fulfillment brings a radical peace, the peace the world cannot give. That fulfillment bears fruit in a love of one's neighbor that strives mightily to bring about the kingdom of God on this earth. On the other hand, the absence of that fulfillment opens the way to the trivialization of human life in the pursuit of fun, to the harshness of human life arising from the ruthless exercise of power, to despair about human welfare springing from the conviction that the universe is absurd. (Lonergan 1972, 105)

Catholicism's basic message is that our lives have great significance and ultimately mean more than we can imagine or even desire in this life. The universe is not absurd; it's just the opposite. Life is full of meaning. All of reality reveals a God who loves us, loves us and saves us. Reducing reality to solely the material makes us miss the truth that there is more and more, much more, to being human than we can hope or imagine. Jesuit scientist and mystic Pierre Teilhard de Chardin more than anyone captures the promise and power of living our Catholic faith as those imbued with the presence and power of the love of God, the message and mission of Jesus, and the transformative fire of the Holy Spirit. "The day will come when, after harnessing space, the winds, the tides, and gravitation, we shall harness for God the energies of love. And on that day, for the second time in the history of the world, the human family shall have discovered fire" (Teilhard de Chardin 1973 [orig. 1934], 86-87).

Acknowledgments

In my first book, I failed to acknowledge several groups of people that should have been recognized. First and foremost, my family and several families, the Ryan clan of Omaha, Nebraska; the Vazquezes of Camden, New Jersey; the Connells of Haddonfield, New Jersey; the Gibsons of Philadelphia; the Morrises of Cody, Wyoming; the Hills of Hockessin, Delaware, and many others have been constant companions and heavenly havens allowing me to experience the joys of family life and learn something of the awesome challenges families face in our days. For fifteen years, the families of Holy Name Parish in North Camden, New Jersey, welcomed me and taught me how to be a priest and a better human being by their joy in life and their courage and perseverance in adversity. For many years, the Sociology Department at Saint Joseph's University in Philadelphia welcomed a cultural anthropologist in their midst, helped me become a university teacher, and supported my efforts to combine research in the social sciences with theological reflection. Also, I owe the greatest debt of my life to the Society of Jesus. Through my brothers in religious life, the Lord saved me from a path of, if not destruction, at least dissipation, and through Jesuit formation brought forth in me talents and abilities I otherwise never would have imagined or realized.

In recent years, many at my new home at the University of Scranton have supported my work as Vice President for University Mission and Ministry. The people of the parish of St. Anthony in Cody, Wyoming, enable me to serve as a chaplain in Yellowstone National Park four Sundays a summer (it's a tough job but someone has to do it!). The beauty and splendor of the West is a wonderful place to write. This book was brought to completion while I was praying and fishing out there in the wilds of Wyoming.

The Sisters of Mercy of Philadelphia, The Sisters of St. Joseph of Chestnut Hill, and the School Sisters of Notre Dame in Baltimore have been great heroes of mine, and they, and all the Sisters in the United States, ought to be so recognized by all in our church. Our Sisters, who taught us when we were little, and who have so admirably and selflessly reached out to the poor and marginalized, should be cherished and honored, not investigated.

The students I've taught over the years and with whom I've interacted in a variety of venues, retreats, clubs, fishing trips, and so on, give me great hope. They will now begin to form the church of the twenty-first century. May the Spirit set them on fire for the Mission.

Portions of chapter 2 appeared first in *U.S. Catholic* (http://www.uscatholic.org/) and *Review for Religious*. Portions of chapter 5 appeared in *Our Sunday Visitor's The Priest Magazine*. Portions of chapter 9 appeared on Bustedhalo.com.

A large debt of gratitude I also owe to Michael Leach and the fine team at Orbis Books. Muchas gracias to all.

August 15, 2013
The Feast of the Assumption.
The University of Scranton, Scranton, Pennsylvania

References

Allen, John L., Jr. 2013. "Right wing 'generally not happy' with Francis, Chaput says." *National Catholic Reporter,* July 23, 2013. http://ncronline.org/blogs/ncr-today/right-wing-generally-not-happy-francis-chaput-says.

Arnold, Johann Christoph. 2010. *Why Forgive?* Maryknoll, NY: Orbis Books.

BabyCenter.com. http://www.babycenter.com/cost-of-raising-child-calculator.

Baldovin, John, S.J. 2003. *Bread of Life, Cup of Salvation.* New York: Rowman & Littlefield.

Barna, George. 2013. "How the Last Decade Changed American Life." July 31, 2013. https://www.barna.org/barna-update/culture/624-how-the-last-decade-changed-american-life#.Ufl211M1DOe.

Basinger, Jeanine. 1986. *It's a Wonderful Life Book.* New York: Knopf.

Benedict XVI [pope; Joseph Ratzinger]. 2007. *Jesus of Nazareth: From the Baptism in the Jordan to the Transfiguration.* New York: Doubleday.

Bergoglio, Jorge Mario. *See* Francis

Berrigan, Daniel, S.J. 1981. *Ten Commandments for the Long Haul: Journeys of Faith.* Nashville, TN: Abingdon Press.

Bochen, Christian M., ed. 2000. "The Hidden Ground of Love." In *Thomas Merton: Essential Writings.* Maryknoll, NY: Orbis Books.

Bogle, Katie. 2007. *Hooking Up: Sex, Dating and Relationships on Campus.* New York: New York University Press.

Bono. 2006. "VERBATIM: In fact the poor are where God lives." *Philadelphia Inquirer,* Sunday, February 26, 2006.

Borg, Marcus. 2006. *Jesus: Uncovering the Life, Teachings, and Relevance of a Religious Revolutionary.* San Francisco: HarperSanFrancisco.

Buechner, Frederick. 1966. *The Magnificent Defeat.* New York: Harper Collins.

Burke, James Lee. 2011. *Feast Day of Fools.* New York: Pocket Books.

Cannato, Judy. 2006. *Radical Amazement: Contemplative Lessons from Black Holes, Supernovas, and Other Wonders of the Universe.* South Bend, IN: Sorin Books.

CARA (Center for Applied Research in the Apostolate, Georgetown University). 2013. "Frequently requested statistics." http://cara.georgetown.edu/CARAServices/requestedchurchstats.html.

Carter, Stephen L. 2002. *The Emperor of Ocean Park.* New York: Random House.

CCC (*Catechism of the Catholic Church*). 1995. New York: Doubleday. See Vatican website: http://www.vatican.va/archive/ENG0015/_INDEX.HTM and USCCB website http://www.usccb.org/beliefs-and-teachings/what-we-believe/catechism/catechism-of-the-catholic-church/epub/index.cfm#.

CNS (Catholic News Service). 2013. "Jesuit superior tells WYD pilgrims 'keep eyes, heart open.'" July 15, 2013. http://www.catholicnews.com/data/stories/cns/1303043.htm.

Connor, James L., S.J. 2006. *The Dynamism of Desire: Bernard J. F. Lonergan, S.J., on the Spiritual Exercises of Saint Ignatius of Loyola.* St. Louis, MO: Institute of Jesuit Sources.

Coyne, George, S.J. 2005. "Infinite Wonder of the Divine." *The Tablet,* December 10, 2005.

Critchley, Simon, and Jamison Webster. "The Gospel According to Me." *New York Times,* June 30, 2013. http://opinionator.blogs.nytimes.com/2013/06/29/the-gospel-according-to-me/.

Delio, Ilia. 2011. *The Emergent Christ: Exploring the Meaning of Catholic in an Evolutionary Universe.* Maryknoll, NY: Orbis Books.

Diamandis, Peter. 2012. "The Future Is Brighter than You Think." CNN, May 6, 2012. http://www.cnn.com/2012/05/06/opinion/diamandis-abundance-innovation.

Dietrich, Jeff. 2011. *Broken and Shared: Food, Dignity, and the Poor on Los Angeles' Skid Row.* Los Angeles: Marymount Institute Press.

Dubus, Andre. 2000. "Sacraments." In *Signatures of Grace: Catholic Writers on the Sacraments,* edited by Thomas Grady and Paula Houston. New York: Dutton.

Farley, Margaret, RSM. 2007. *Just Love: A Framework for Christian Social Ethics.* New York: Continuum.

Francis (pope). 2013. "The Humblest Offer the World a Lesson in Solidarity." World Youth Day, Rio de Janeiro, Brazil, July 25, 2013. http://www.news.va/en/news/pope-francis-the-humblest-offer-the-world-a-lesson.

George, Francis Cardinal, O.M.I. 2009. *The Difference God Makes: A Catholic Vision of Faith Communion and Culture.* New York: Crossroad.

Goldsmith, Donald. 1991. *The Astronomers.* Companion Book to the PBS Television Series. New York: St. Martin's Press.

Greene, Brian. 2004. *The Fabric of the Cosmos: Space, Time, and the Texture of Reality.* New York: Vintage Books.

———. 2011. "Darkness on the Edge of the Universe." *New York Times,* January 15, 2011. http://www.nytimes.com/2011/01/16/opinion/16greene.html?_r=1&scp=3&sq=brian+greene&st=nyt.

Hawking, Stephen. 2001. *The Universe in a Nutshell.* New York: Bantam Books.

Heagle, John. 2010. *Justice Rising: The Emerging Biblical Vision.* Maryknoll, NY: Orbis Books.

Hillenbrand, Laura. 2010. *Unbroken: A World War II Story of Survival, Resilience and Redemption.* New York: Random House.

Horsley, Richard A., and Neil Asher Silberman. 1997. *The Message and the Kingdom: How Jesus and Paul Ignited a Revolution and Transformed the Ancient World.* New York: Grosset/Putnam.

Ilibagiza, Immaculée. 2007. *Left to Tell: Discovering God Amidst the Rwandan Holocaust.* Carlsbad, CA: Hay House.

John Paul II (pope). 1987. Quoting United States' Bishops 1986 "Economic Justice for All" in an address to Catholic Charities, California, September 19, 1987. In *The Wisdom of John Paul II: The Pope on Life's Most Vital Questions,* edited by Nick Bakalar and Richard Balkin. San Francisco: HarperSanFrancisco, 1995.

Kennedy, Paul. 2013. "Which Catholic Church?" *New York Times*, Op-ed page, February 27, 2013. http://www.nytimes. com/2013/02/27/opinion/global/which-catholic-church. html?pagewanted=all&_r=0.

King, Rev. Martin Luther, Jr. 1967. "A Christmas Sermon on Peace." Ebenezer Baptist Church, Christmas Eve, 1967. http://www. ecoflourish.com/Primers/education/Christmas_Sermon.html.

Kristof, Nicholas. 2011. "America's Primal Scream." *New York Times*, Op-ed page, October 15, 2011. http://www.nytimes. com/2011/10/16/opinion/sunday/kristof-americas-primal-scream.html.

———. 2012. "Why Let the Rich Hoard All the Toys?" *New York Times*, Op-ed page, October 3, 2012. http://www.nytimes. com/2012/10/04/opinion/kristof-why-let-the-rich-hoard-all-the-toys.html?_r=0.

Kristof, Nicholas D., and Sheryl WuDunn. 2009. *Half the Sky: Turning Oppression into Opportunity for Women Worldwide.* New York: Vintage Books. http://www.halftheskymovement.org/

Krugman, Paul. 2013. "Hunger Games U.S.A." *New York Times,* Op-ed page, July 14, 2013. http://www.nytimes.com/2013/07/15/ opinion/krugman-hunger-games-usa.html?_r=0.

Lamott, Anne. 2005. *Plan B: Further Thoughts on Faith.* New York: Riverhead Books.

Lawrie, Bruce. 2009. "Who Am I, Lord, That You Should Know My Name." *Portland Magazine,* http://www.up.edu/portland-mag/2009_summer/whoami.htm.

Lindbergh, Anne Morrow. 1975. *Gift from the Sea.* New York: Pantheon Books. First published 1955.

Livingston, Patricia. 2006. *Let in the Light.* Notre Dame, IN: Sorin Books.

Lohfink, Gerhard. 2012. *Jesus of Nazareth: What He Wanted and Who He Was.* Collegeville, MN: Liturgical Press.

Lonergan, Bernard, S.J. 1972. *Method in Theology.* Toronto: University of Toronto Press.

Luhrmann, T. M. 2013. "The Benefits of Church." *New York Times,* April 20, 2013. http://www.nytimes.com/2013/04/21/opinion/sunday/luhrmann-why-going-to-church-is-good-for-you.html?_r=0.

Malloy, Richard G., S.J. 2008. *A Faith That Frees: Catholic Matters for the 21st Century.* Maryknoll, NY: Orbis Books.

Massingale, Bryan. 2013. "Diversity on the Jesuit Campus." An address to the Association of Jesuit Colleges and Universities Leadership Seminar. Loyola University, Chicago, June, 21, 2013.

McBrien, Richard. 1981. *Catholicism: Study Edition.* Minneapolis: Winston Press.

Meier, John P. 1994. *A Marginal Jew: Rethinking the Historical Jesus.* Volume 2, *Mentor, Message, and Miracles.* Anchor Bible Reference Library. New York: Doubleday.

Merton, Thomas. 1956. *The Living Bread.* New York: Farrar, Straus & Giroux.

Morris, Richard. 1990. *The Edges of Science.* Upper Saddle River, NJ: Prentice Hall.

Neihardt, John G. 1972. *Black Elk Speaks.* New York: Pocket Books.

"Overpaid? Or Worth Every Penny?" *New York Times,* editorial, July 13, 2013. http://www.nytimes.com/2013/07/14/opinion/sunday/overpaid-or-worth-every-penny.html?ref=editorials&pagewanted=print.

Pagola, Jose Antonio. 2012. *Jesus: An Historical Approximation.* Miami: Convivium Press. First published 2007.

Pew Forum. 2008. "U.S. Religious Landscape Survey: Religious Affiliation Diverse and Dynamic. Feb 2008." http://religions.pewforum.org/pdf/report-religious-landscape-study-full.pdf and http://religions.pewforum.org/reports.

Pilch, John J. 1995. *The Cultural World of Jesus: Sunday by Sunday, Cycle A.* Collegeville, MN: Liturgical Press.

Powers, William K. 1977. *Oglala Religion.* Lincoln: University of Nebraska Press.

Privett, Stephen, S.J. 2003. "The View from Outside." *Conversations on Jesuit Higher Education,* vol. 23, article 4.

Rahner, Karl, S.J. 1966. "The Theology of the Symbol." In *Theological Investigations.* Volume 4, *More Recent Writings,* 221-52. Translated by Kevin Smyth. Baltimore: Helicon Press; London: Darton, Longman & Todd.

———. 1967. "The Comfort of Time." In *Theological Investigations.* Volume 3, *The Theology of the Spiritual Life,* 141-60. Translated by Karl-H. Kruger and Boniface Kruger. Baltimore: Helicon Press; London: Darton, Longman & Todd.

Ratzinger, Joseph. *See* Benedict XVI

Rausch, Thomas P., S.J. 2010. *Educating for Faith and Justice: Catholic Higher Education Today.* Collegeville, MN: Liturgical Press.

Ravizza, Mark, S.J. 2010. "Praxis Based Education." In Thomas P. Rausch, S.J., *Educating for Faith and Justice: Catholic Higher Education Today,* 111-26. Collegeville, MN: Liturgical Press.

Rohr, Richard. 2003. *Everything Belongs: The Gift of Contemplative Prayer.* New York: Crossroad.

Romero, Óscar. 1998. *The Violence of Love,* compiled and translated by James R. Brockman, S.J. Farmington, PA: Plough. www.plough.com. First published 1988.

Rooney, Eugene, S.J. "Bud." 2013. *Chile Report Today #45.* Baltimore: Jesuit Maryland Province Offices.

Ryan, Br. Dennis Jude, S.J. 1990. "MY TURN: 'Why Be a Brother?' To Foster Gospel Values." *Twin Cities Catholic Newspaper.*

Saenz, Rogelio. 2005. "The Changing Demographics of Roman Catholics." http://www.prb.org/Articles/2005/TheChanging-DemographicsofRomanCatholics.aspx.

Sagan, Carl. 1977. *The Dragons of Eden.* New York: Ballentine Books.

Sandel, Michael J. 2009. *Justice: What's the Right Thing to Do?* New York: Farrar, Straus & Giroux.

Smith, Christian, Kari Christoffersen, Hilary Davidson, and Patricia Snell Herzog. 2011. *Lost in Transition: The Dark Side of Emerging Adulthood*. New York: Oxford University Press.

Smith, Christian, and Patricia Snell. 2009. *Souls in Transition: The Religious and Spiritual Lives of Emerging Adults*. New York: Oxford University Press.

Spitzer, Robert J., S.J. 2010. *New Proofs for the Existence of God: Contributions of Contemporary Physics and Philosophy*. Grand Rapids: Eerdmans.

Stanley, David M., S.J. 1967. *A Modern Scriptural Approach to the Spiritual Exercises*. Chicago: The Institute of Jesuit Sources in cooperation with Loyola University Press.

Steinmetz, Paul B., S.J. 1988. *Pipe, Bible and Peyote among the Oglala Lakota: A Study in Religious Identity*. Syracuse, NY: Syracuse University Press. First published 1980.

Steltenkamp, Michael F., S.J. 1993. *Black Elk: Holy Man of the Oglala*. Norman: University of Oklahoma Press.

Stiglitz, Joseph E. 2013a. *The Price of Inequality: How Today's Divided Society Endangers Our Future*. New York: W. W. Norton.

———.2013b. "A Tax System Stacked against the 99%." *New York Times*, April 14, 2013. http://opinionator.blogs.nytimes.com/2013/04/14/a-tax-system-stacked-against-the-99-percent/.

Svaldi, Aldo. 2013. "Why Exec Pay Seems Too High." *Denver Post*, June 30, 2013, 3K.

Taylor, Charles. 2007. *A Secular Age*. Cambridge, MA: Belknap Press of Harvard University Press.

Teilhard de Chardin, Pierre, S.J. 1973. "The Evolution of Chastity." In *Toward the Future*. New York: Harcourt Brace Jovanovich. First published 1934. See http://teilharddechardin.org/index.php/teilhards-quotes.

———. 2002. *The Phenomenon of Man*. New York: Harper Perennial Modern Classic. First published 1955. See http://en.wikiquote.org/wiki/Pierre_Teilhard_de_Chardin.

Tier, Julia. "Sex and the University: How Does the Church Speak to the Experience of Younger Catholics?" January 29, 2004. http://bustedhalo.com/features/sex-and-the-university.

USCCB (United States Conference of Catholic Bishops). 1986. "Economic Justice for All." http://www.usccb.org/upload/economic_justice_for_all.pdf.

———. 2005-6. "Charter for the Protection of Children and Young People" and "Essential Norms for Diocesan/Eparchial Policies Dealing with Allegations of Sexual Abuse of Minors by Priests or Deacons." Washington, DC. http://old.usccb.org/ocyp/charter.pdf; http://www.usccb.org/issues-and-action/child-and-youth-protection/upload/Charter-for-the-Protection-of-Children-and-Young-People-revised-2011.pdf.

———. 2011. "The Causes and Context of Sexual Abuse of Minors by Catholic Priests in the United States, 1950-2010: A Report Presented to the United States Conference of Catholic Bishops by the John Jay College Research Team." http://www.usccb.org/issues-and-action/child-and-youth-protection/upload/The-Causes-and-Context-of-Sexual-Abuse-of-Minors-by-Catholic-Priests-in-the-United-States-1950-2010.pdf.

U.S. Census. 2012. "Income, Poverty and Health Insurance Coverage in the United States: 2011." http://www.census.gov/newsroom/releases/archives/income_wealth/cb12-172.html.

Vanier, Jean. 2008. "Our Journey Home." In *Jean Vanier: Essential Writings*. Maryknoll, NY: Orbis Books.

Ward, Donald Malcolm, S.J. 2009. In *Ignatian Imprints*, vol. 3, no. 4. A Publication of the Maryland Province Jesuits. http://www.mdsj.org/IgnImp/IgnatianImprintsSummer09.pdf.

Weekly, Chris, S.J. 1994. "Holy Rosary" (account of the death, wake, and funeral of Br. Dennis Ryan, S.J.) in Wisconsin Province of the Society of Jesus, *News*, vol. XXXVI, no. 5. May-June 1994. Milwaukee, WI: Provincial's Offices. Pp. 1-3.

Wingert, Pat. 2010. "Mean Men: The priesthood is being cast as the refuge of pederasts. In fact, priests seem to abuse children at the same rate as everyone else." *The Daily Beast*, April 7, 2010. http://www.thedailybeast.com/newsweek/2010/04/07/mean-men.html.

Wooden, Cindy. 2013. "Statistically Speaking: Vatican Numbers Hint at Fading Faith Practice." Catholic News Service, http://www. catholicnews.com/data/stories/cns/1203473.htm.

World Bank. 2013. "Poverty." http://web.worldbank.org/WBSITE/ EXTERNAL/TOPICS/EXTPOVERTY/EXTPA/0,,content MDK:20040961~menuPK:435040~pagePK:148956~piPK:2 16618~theSitePK:430367~isCURL:Y,00.html.

Worthen, Molly. 2012. "One Nation under God." *New York Times*, Sunday Review, Opinion pages, December 22, 2012. http:// www.nytimes.com/2012/12/23/opinion/sunday/american-christianity-and-secularism-at-a-crossroads.html.

Wright, N. T. 1999. *The Challenge of Jesus: Rediscovering Who Jesus Was and Who He Is*. Downers Grove, IL: InterVarsity Press.

———. 2011. *Simply Jesus: A New Vision of Who He Was, What He Did, and Why He Matters*. New York: HarperOne.

Wu, Emily. 2004. "Meeting Fr. Zhang." *America Magazine*, vol. 190, no. 13, April 12, 2004. http://americamagazine.org/issue/481/ faith-focus/meeting-father-zhang.

Yen, Hope. 2012. "U.S. Poverty on Track to Rise to Highest since 1960s." July 22, 2012. http://www.huffingtonpost.com/2012/ 07/22/us-poverty-level-1960s_n_1692744.html.

Zakaria, Fareed. 2008. *The Post-American World*. New York: W. W. Norton.

Recommended Reading

1. God Loves us

Lawrie, Bruce. 2009. "Who Am I, Lord, That You Should Know My Name." *Portland Magazine,* http://www.up.edu/portland-mag/2009_summer/whoami.htm.

Tierney, Dana. 2004. "Coveting Luke's Faith." *New York Times Magazine*, January 11, 2004. http://www.nytimes.com/2004/01/11/magazine/11LIVES.html.

Wu, Emily. 2004. "Meeting Fr. Zhang." *America Magazine*, vol. 190, no. 13, April 12, 2004. http://americamagazine.org/issue/481/faith-focus/meeting-father-zhang.

2. Creation, and All in It, Is Good, Very Good

Coyne, George, S.J.. 2005. "Infinite Wonder of the Divine." *The Tablet*, December 10, 2005.

Rohr, Richard, OFM. 2003. *Everything Belongs: The Gift of Contemplative Prayer.* New York: Crossroad.

3. Jesus: The Essential Gift

Borg, Marcus. 2006. *Jesus: Uncovering the Life, Teachings, and Relevance of a Religious Revolutionary.* San Francisco: HarperSanFrancisco.

Dear, John, S.J. 2004. *The Questions of Jesus: Challenging Ourselves to Discover Life's Great Answers.* New York: Doubleday, Image Books.

Mailer, Norman. 1997. *The Gospel According to the Son.* New York: Ballentine.

Wright, N. T. 2011. *Simply Jesus: A New Vision of Who He Was, What He Did, and Why He Mattters*. New York: HarperOne.

4. Christ Is Community

Kennedy, Paul. 2013. "Which Catholic Church?" *New York Times*, Op-ed page, February 27, 2013. http://www.nytimes.com/2013/02/27/opinion/global/which-catholic-church.html?pagewanted=all&_r=0.
Leach, Michael. 2011. *Why Stay Catholic? Unexpected Answers to a Life-Changing Question*. Chicago: Loyola University Press.

5. The Church: Both Divine and Human

Lonergan, Bernard J. F., S.J. 1985. "The Dialectic of Authority." In *A Third Collection*, edited by Frederick Crowe, S.J., 5-12. Mahwah, NJ: Paulist Press.
Sobrino, Jon, S.J. 1984. *The True Church and the Poor*. Maryknoll, NY: Orbis Books.

6. Righting Relationships: The Work of Justice and Forgiveness

Dietrich, Jeff. 2011. *Broken and Shared: Food, Dignity, and the Poor on Los Angeles' Skid Row*. Los Angeles: Marymount Institute Press.
Ilibagiza, Immaculée. 2007. *Left to Tell: Discovering God Amidst the Rwandan Holocaust*. Carlsbad, CA: Hay House.

7. Sacraments Sing Our Stories

Dubus, Andre. 2000. "Sacraments." In *Signatures of Grace: Catholic Writers on the Sacraments*, edited by Thomas Grady and Paula Houston. New York: Dutton.
Knipper, James J., ed. 2012. *Hungry and You Fed Me: Homilies and Reflections for Cycle C*. Manalapan, NJ: Clear Vision.

Pungente, John, S.J., and Monty Williams, S.J. 2004. *Finding God in the Dark: Taking the Spiritual Exercises of St. Ignatius to the Movies*. Boston: Pauline Books and Media; Toronto: Novalis.

8. Mission Matters. Jesus says, "Come on, we're going to change the World"

Gallagher, Vincent. 2013. *The True Cost of Low Prices: The Violence of Globalization*. Maryknoll, NY: Orbis Books.
Heagle, John. 2010. *Justice Rising: The Emerging Biblical Vision*. Maryknoll, NY: Orbis Books.

9. Practice Makes Us Better, Not Perfect

Arnold, Johann Christoph. 2010. *Why Forgive?* Maryknoll, NY: Orbis Books.
Rohr, Richard, OFM. 2011. *Falling Upward: A Spirituality for the Two Halves of Life*. San Francisco: Jossey-Bass.

10. Smile: Despite It All, the Universe Is User-Friendly

Malloy, Richard G., S.J. 2013. "Mind Your 'P's. Presence, Praise, Process, Penance and Promise: St. Ignatius' Examen Provides Exercise for the Soul." *St. Anthony Messenger*, February 2013, 40-44. http://www.americancatholic.org/samo/Feature.aspx?article id=143&IssueID=45.
Romero, Óscar. 1998. *The Violence of Love: The Pastoral Wisdom of Archbishop Oscar Romero*, compiled and translated by James R. Brockman, S.J. Farmington, PA: Plough. www.plough.com. First published 1988.